Dublin
CITY OF LITERATURE

MURIEL BOLGER

DUBLIN
UNESCO
City of Literature

THE O'BRIEN PRESS
DUBLIN

First published 2011 by
The O'Brien Press Ltd,
12 Terenure Road East,
Rathgar, Dublin 6, Ireland.
Tel: +353 1 4923333; Fax: +353 1
4922777
E-mail: books@obrien.ie
Website: www.obrien.ie

ISBN: 978-1-84717-248-8

1 2 3 4 5 6 7 8 9 10
11 12 13 14 15

Typesetting, layout, editing, design:
The O'Brien Press Ltd
Printed and bound by
GPS Colour Graphics, Belfast

The paper in this book is produced using
pulp from managed forests.

An Roinn
Ealaíon, Oidhreachta agus Gaeltachta
Department of
Arts, Heritage and the Gaeltacht

Tá an tionscadal seo páirt-mhaoinithe
ag An Roinn Ealaíon, Oidhreachta agus
Gaeltachta.
This project has been part-funded by the
Department of Arts, Heritage and the
Gaeltacht.

JAMES
JOYCE
1882-1941

Bust of James Joyce in
St Stephen's Green
Crossing Stephen's
that is my green...

Contents

McDaids Pub, 3 Harry Street, frequented by Brendan Behan, Parick Kavanagh et al.

The recognition of Dublin as UNESCO City of Literature was both appropriate and timely, as is the production of this volume. Any representative roll call of English literature, or perhaps I should say literature in the English language, will inevitably reveal a rich seam of Irishness. Irish writers have for centuries been to the forefront in the fields of drama, poetry and prose. Swift, Joyce, Beckett, Yeats, Wilde, Synge, O'Casey, Shaw, Behan right up to contemporaries such as Dermot Bolger, Roddy Doyle and Colum McCann. Every time one imagines the list closed new names spring to mind.

The reasons for this are complex and one of them certainly is what was for many people a heartbreaking transition from the ancient Gaelic language into the more practical vehicle of English. Joyce was not alone when in *A Portrait* he has Stephen Dedalus say, 'My soul frets in the shadow of his language'. Yet this sadness, this irritation, this grating of one system of expression and feeling against one another and the conflict between the rational imperial language of Britain and the sometimes more subtle evasive structures of the Irish language proved fertile in producing a people with a separate identity and a fresh and subversive attitude towards language, not only its meaning but its variety, texture, shape and sound.

Many Dublin writers, most particularly Joyce, give special and detailed attention to the city, and Bloomsday, the celebration of the day in which Joyce's redaction of Homer's *Odyssey* into the 20th century novel *Ulysses*, has for many years featured walking tours of sites associated with the novel. The city is literally pockmarked with plaques on buildings marking the fact that some literary celebrity lived, died or worked there. This also facilitates a variety of other walking tours, some combined with convivial visits to Dublin hostelries, and a number are available to the tourist on a year round basis. Helpful suggestions are made in this book in addition for do-it-yourself walks around the city of Dublin.

This entertaining and fact-filled book will make a valuable companion for any visitor – or indeed local – interested in Dublin's literary heritage.

Senator David Norris

The City of Literature award is part of the UNESCO Creative Cities Network launched in 2004.

Dublin is one of only four cities in the world with the designation of UNESCO: City of Literature, joining Edinburgh, Melbourne and Iowa City on the list.

The sought-after accolade, which is permanent, recognises Dublin's cultural profile and its international standing as a city of literary excellence.

Jane Alger – Director, Dublin UNESCO City of Literature:

Words are part of what we are in Dublin, and 'What's the story?' is a standard greeting among Dubliners. Everything starts with words, the way words are used in Dublin. Words are the basis of stories; stories lead to writing - writing in all its forms - novels, prose, poetry, drama, song writing, comedy…

You can hear the words used by Dubliners in writing by Dubliners, in Joyce's *Dubliners*, in the novels of Paul Murray, Roddy Doyle, Patricia Scanlan and so many more. Words written by Patrick Kavanagh have been set to music and sung by the Dubliners. Bagatelle sang about summer in Dublin. The fact that words are so important to life in Dublin may explain the respect and affection in which writers are held, and their names appear everywhere – on streets, bridges and ships, and in quotes from their works in Dublin Airport.

Literature is part of Dublin, and Dublin is part of literature.

DUBLIN
UNESCO
City of Literature

John Banville
Author of *The Sea*, Man Booker winner 2005.

'Since the days of Jonathan Swift, Edmund Burke and Oliver Goldsmith to the present time of the Nobel Laureate Seamus Heaney and Man Booker prize-winner Anne Enright, Dublin has had a continuing, rich and vital literary life. I believe that it is only fitting that this living tradition should be recognised by UNESCO.'

John Connolly
Bestselling author of the *Charlie Parker* crime thriller series.

'It's always tempting to fall back on the great names of the past who have walked the streets of this city, and whose spirits continue to infuse so much of the literary life of this city, and those names in themselves would be enough to merit Dublin's consideration for this honour. But a City of Literature should not merely resemble a UNESCO heritage site: it's not enough that, once upon a time, greatness and beauty might have occupied a place in the world, and some relic of that greatness and beauty remains and continues to resonate with us. What is important in a City of Literature is that it remains as vibrant as it ever was. It should not simply hold the echoes, however strong, of the voices that once spoke universal truths in it, and about it. Instead, those voices should, in turn, have inspired others to come forward, and to raise their voices in turn. Dublin is such a city, and I am proud to play my small part in its great literary tradition.'

Irvine Welsh
Edinburgh-born writer, author of *Trainspotting*, who adopted Dublin as his sometimes home.

'Dublin is a city brimming with stories, the local and the international, provided by incomers and the returning members of the Irish diaspora. It's difficult to think of any place on the globe more appropriate for the UNESCO City of Literature designation.'

What the writers say ●●●●●

BEWLEY'S ORIENTAL CAFES LTD

Bewley's cafe, formerly the site of Samuel Whyte's Academy, alma mater of Richard Brinsley Sheridan, Isaac Weld, Arthur Wellesley, the Duke of Wellington

1667 Jonathan Swift, creator of *Gulliver's Travels* and Dean of St Patrick's Cathedral, is born

1701 Marsh's Library, the first public library, opens beside St Patrick's Cathedral

1728 Oliver Goldsmith is born

1751 Richard Brinsley Sheridan, poet, playwright and owner of Drury Lane Theatre, London, is born

1814 Joseph Sheridan Le Fanu, writer of Gothic tales and mystery novels, is born

1820 Dion Boucicault, actor and playwright, is born

1847 Bram Stoker, creator of *Dracula*, is born

1854 Oscar Wilde, wit, playwright and poet, is born

1856 George Bernard Shaw, playwright and author of *Pygmalion*, is born

1865 William Butler Yeats, poet and driving force behind the Irish Literary Revival and co-founder of the Abbey Theatre, is born

1871 John Millington Synge, playwright and poet, is born

1880 Sean O'Casey, playwright, is born

1882 James Joyce, author of *Ulysses*, *Dubliners* and *Finnegan's Wake*, is born

1896 Austin Clarke, poet, is born

1904 The Abbey Theatre is founded by Lady Gregory, William Butler Yeats and Edward Martyn

1906 Samuel Beckett, writer of *Waiting for Godot*, is born

1907 Riots break out over the production of Synge's *Playboy of the Western World* at the Abbey Theatre

1910 Máirtín Ó Direáin, poet, is born

1916 Poets and Republicans Patrick Pearse, Joseph Plunkett and Thomas MacDonagh are executed for their part in the Easter Rising

1917 Poet Francis Ledwidge killed in action at Passchendale during WW1

1922 Joyce's *Ulysses* is published by Sylvia Beach in Paris on 2 February

1923 Brendan Behan of *Borstal Boy* fame is born

1925 George Bernard Shaw awarded the Nobel Prize for Literature

1926 Sean O'Casey's *The Plough and the Stars* causes riots at the Abbey Theatre

1928 Gate Theatre founded by Hilton Edwards and Micheál MacLiammóir

1929 Frank O'Connor, master of the short story, is appointed librarian to the newly opened Pembroke Library on Anglesea Road, Ballsbridge

1931 James Joyce marries his long-time partner Nora Barnacle

1938 *My Fair Lady*, written by George Bernard Shaw as *Pygmalion*, receives an Oscar for Best Writing, Screenplay

1940 The literary journal *The Bell*, is founded by Sean O'Faoláin

1941 James Joyce dies in Switzerland and is buried in Fluntern Cemetery in Zurich

1944 Poet Paul Durcan is born

1946 George Bernard Shaw is made a Freeman of Dublin city

1948 Brian O'Nolan, aka Flann O'Brien/Myles na gCopaleen marries Evelyn McDonnell

1949 Jim Sheridan, screenwriter and director whose work includes *My Left Foot*, is born

1954, 16 June, Ireland holds its first Bloomsday celebrations, marking the 50th anniversary of Leopold Bloom's walk through Dublin in Joyce's *Ulysses*

1957 Dublin Theatre Festival launched. Director of the Pike Theatre is arrested for staging of *The Rose Tattoo*

1961 James Plunkett, who wrote *Strumpet City*, is appointed a director of Ireland's first national television station

1965 Lee Dunne's *Goodbye to the Hill* is published. The book is banned in Ireland.

1969 Samuel Beckett is awarded the Nobel Prize for Literature

1971 John Boyne, author of *The Boy in the Striped Pyjamas,* is born

1973 Elizabeth Bowen, who wrote *Seven Winters, Memories of a Dublin Childhood*, dies

1976 Eavan Boland wins the Irish Jacob's Award for Poetry

1979 Jennifer Johnstons's *Old Jest* wins the Booker Prize

1981 James Clarence Mangan's gravestone is inscribed with lines from his poem *My Dark Rosaleen*, some thirty-two years after his death

1982 Maeve Binchy's first novel *Light a Penny Candle*, is published

1985 The National Print

Museum opens at the former Garrison Chapel in Beggars Bush

1988 Máire Mhac an tSaoi wins the O'Shaughnessy Poetry Award of the Irish American Cultural Institute

1990 Bisto Children's Book Awards are established

1990 Paul Durcan wins the Whitbread Poetry Award

1992 The film adaptation of Roddy Doyle's *The Commitments* wins a BAFTA Award

1993 Roddy Doyle wins the Booker Prize for *Paddy Clarke Ha Ha Ha*

1995 Seamus Heaney is awarded the Nobel Prize for Literature

1995 The IMPAC Dublin Literary award – the world's richest fiction prize – is launched

2000 The first Dublin Writers Festival is launched

2001 Michael Hartnett' s *Collected Poems* is published posthumously

2004 IMRAM, the Irish Language Theatre Festival, is launched

2005 John Banville wins the Man Booker award for his novel *The Sea*

2006 The award-winning Dublin: One City One Book initiative is established

2006 The Irish Book Awards are launched. Conor McPherson gets a Tony nomination for *Shining City* and an Olivier Award nomination for Best New Play for *The Seafarer*.

2007 Thomas Kinsella is given the Honorary Freedom of the City for his contribution to the cultural heritage of Dublin

2007 Anne Enright wins the Man Booker Prize with *The Gathering*

2008 Sebastian Barry wins the Costa Book of the Year Award

2009 Marian Keyes wins an Irish Book Award for her popular fiction

2009 Colum McCann wins the fiction prize in the US National Book Awards for *Let the Great World Spin*

2010 Dublin is conferred with the UNESCO designation as City of Literature.

The Writers

Past and Present

The writers in this book include those who were born, lived, were educated in, wrote or worked in Dublin, as well as those who adopted Dublin temporarily or permanently. It features many who struggled, emigrated or were exiled from the city and includes others whose works, great and small, have made Dublin live on in all its guises, with all its flaws and charms utterly exposed.

No matter where you go in the city today there are remnants and traces of many of these writers - in the places where they lived, wrote, drank, gathered, or socialised.

The list is by no means comprehensive, but compiled to show a diversity of the writers who have walked the cobbles of the capital since the days of Jonathan Swift, breathing in the essences that helped make Dublin a City of Words – a City of Literature.

It would have been impossible to list everyone, and to those writers I have omitted I offer my genuine apologies.

Muriel Bolger

A-L

AE George Russell
1867-1935

Lurgan-born George Russell (AE) moved to Dublin when his father got work here. The family lived in 33 Emorville Avenue for several years and George went to Power's School in Harrington Street, then to Dr C W Benson's Rathmines School, and then on to the Metropolitan School of Art in Kildare Street (now the National College of Art and Design in Thomas Street) continuing in night classes after he got a job as a draper's clerk in what was once Dublin's largest department store, Messrs Pim Brothers on South Great George's Street. The family moved to 67 Grosvenor Square and George began attending meetings of the Theosophical Society, eventually moving in to their premises at 3 Upper Ely Place. It was around this time that he started calling himself AE, a pseudonym by which he is best remembered. It has its origins in the word AEON, but this was a little complicated for the compositor who was typesetting his work, so he simply dropped the last two letters and used the AE instead.

AE witnessed the blossoming of the Irish Literary Society whose goals – to foster and promote a new school of literature for the Irish (although not written in the vernacular) appealed to him. He joined the Irish Agricultural Organisation Society and worked very closely with its founder, Sir Horace Plunkett, becoming editor of the *Irish Homestead*, which published weekly from 1895 to1923, and subsequently its replacement, the *Irish Statesman*. It was in the former that James Joyce's *Eveline* and *Sisters* first appeared under his pseudonym Stephen Dedalus and in the latter that AE published Kavanagh, Yeats, Frank O'Connor and Shaw, among others. He met his wife, Violet, while living at Ely Place. They moved from 10 Grove Terrace to 6 Castlewood Avenue, and on to 28 Upper Mount Pleasant Avenue, all in a matter of months before finally nesting for a few years at 25 Coulson Avenue, Rathgar. There they had interesting neighbours – Count and Countess Markievicz, while Maud Gonne lived next door – a virtual Celtic Revival on one avenue. The Russells moved to 17 Rathgar Avenue, where they spent twenty-five years. Their house became known for its gatherings, where the literary circuit of those days congregated to exchange ideas and opinions. Frequent

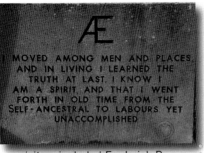

MOVED AMONG MEN AND PLACES,
AND IN LIVING I LEARNED THE
TRUTH AT LAST. I KNOW I
AM A SPIRIT AND THAT I WENT
FORTH IN OLD TIME FROM THE
SELF-ANCESTRAL TO LABOURS YET
UNACCOMPLISHED

visitors included Frederick R Higgins, Frank O'Connor, Austin Clarke, Padraic Colum, Francis Ledwidge, Seumus O'Sullivan and many more.

His wife wrote one book, *Heroes of the Dawn*. Following her death, after thirty-four years of marriage, AE moved to London. He died in Bournemouth three years later and was returned to Ireland to be buried in Mount Jerome Cemetery, Harold's Cross.

A commemorative bust by sculptor Jerome O'Connor (*see opposite*) is located on the west side of Merrion Square, close to AE'S office with the Irish Agricultural Organisation Society.

As well as writing plays, poetry and fiction, AE wrote on mysticism, politics, and economics. His novels are *The Interpreters* and *The Avatars*; his poetry includes *Gods of War with Other Poems*, *Imaginations and Reveries*, *The Candle of Vision*, *Autobiography of a Mystic*, *Midsummer Eve* and *Enchantment and Other Poems*.

Ivy Bannister
1951-

Born in New York, but living in Dublin for many years, Bannister did her PhD in Trinity College. She writes poetry, short stories, plays, among them *The Wilde Circus Show*, which have been produced on radio and stage in Ireland and elsewhere, and has also written a memoir, *Blunt Trauma*. She is a frequent contributor to radio miscellany programmes. Bannister has won many awards for her writings, including the OZ Whitehead Play, Best Play, Listowel Festival, the PJ O'Connor and Francis MacManus Awards. She lives in Stillorgan, Co Dublin.

John Banville
1945-

Wexford-born John Banville worked in the now defunct *Irish Press* in Dublin and subsequently in *The Irish Times* as a sub editor and eventually as literary editor. His first book of short stories appeared as *Long Lankin* and was

published in 1970, followed the next year by a novel *Nightspawn*. Over the years he has become a regular award winner for his writings. *The Book of Evidence* was shortlisted for the Booker Prize in 1989; he won that coveted award in 2005 with *The Sea*. That also snapped up the Irish Book Awards Novel of the Year in 2006. He has written several plays and, using the pen name Benjamin Black, he writes crime novels that include *Christine Falls* and *Elegy for April*. With producer and actress Glenn Close, he recently co-wrote the screenplay for George Moore's short story *The Singular Life of Albert Nobbs*, which was filmed in Dublin.

Mary Barber
c.1685-c.1755

Poet Mary Barber was born on Capel Street where her father had a drapery shop. She was a member of Jonathan Swift's inner circle – the 'female senate' – where she was known as *Sapphira*. He described her as 'a virtuous modest gentlewoman, with a great deal of good sense' and she enjoyed his sponsorship, which was to cost her dearly. She was arrested for bringing six of his poems, supposedly with subversive content, into England. For her troubles she was sent to jail for fourteen days. In 1734 she came to notice when she was awarded one guinea, a vast sum, for a collection of poems – *Poems on Several Occasions*, which went out to a subscription list of 918 of her followers.

Lines from Barber's *An Unanswerable Apology for the Rich* include:

How do our hearts deceive us here!
He gets ten thousand Pounds a Year.
With this the pious Youth is able
To build, and plant, and keep a table.
But then the Poor he must not treat:
Who asks the Wretch, that wants to eat?
Alas! To ease their Woes he wishes,
But cannot live without Ten Dishes,
Tho' Six would serve as well,'tis true:
But one must live, as others do.

Jonah Barrington
1760-1834

Jonah Barrington left us with some very amusing and insightful accounts of life and society in his often scathing but humorous sketches of contemporary Irish lawyers, judges and politicians. There are three volumes of these *Personal Sketches of his Own Times*.

Barrington was born in Co Laois but brought to Dublin as a child. His family was very aware of status and his mother was full of ostentation. She flitted from one social engagement to another in a gilded carriage drawn by four jet-black horses and carrying two postilions. Jonah attended Trinity College and was called to the Bar before taking silk in 1793. Five years later he was appointed as Admiralty Court Judge. His wife came with a large dowry enabling them to buy 12, now 14 Harcourt Street. The house had a large window that was blocked up and then re-installed as its position caused friction between the Barringtons and their immediate neighbours, Lord and Lady Clonmel, who felt they were being spied on. Every afternoon Mrs Barrington settled there in her finery to watch the goings and comings on the street and next-door. Barrington opposed the act of Union and eventually moved to France to avoid his creditors and the accusations against him for fiddling the court funds.

Sebastian Barry
1955-

Sebastian Barry was born in Dublin. He was educated at the Catholic University School and Trinity College, where he edited the college literary magazine *Icarus*. His novels have twice been nominated for the Man Booker Prize - in 2005 for *A Long Long Way* and in 2008 for *The Secret Scripture*, for which he won the Costa Book of the Year. Barry has also written numerous plays including *The Pride of Parnell Street*, *Whistling Psyche*, *Tales of Ballycumber* and *Andersen's English*. He has two collections of poetry: *The Water Colourist* and *The Rhetorical Town*.

Henrietta Battier
c.1751-1813

Meath-born poet Henrietta Battier spent much of her life in Dublin. It appears that she didn't take herself too seriously, prefacing her first volume of poetry, published in 1791, *The Protected Fugitives: a collection of miscellaneous poems, the genuine products of a lady, never before published*, with the words 'a better housewife than a poet'. Her works charmed, amused and diverted a wide audience and the proceeds went towards swelling the depleted family coffers. She regarded poet and bard Thomas Moore as a friend and he was a frequent visitor to her lodgings in Fade Street, Dublin 2. Despite her popularity and having supposedly earned the princely sum of 915 guineas for a collected work, she died in poverty in Sandymount.

Photo: Photocall Ireland

Samuel Beckett
1906-89

Beckett grew up in Foxrock, in a house called Cooldrinagh. He was educated at Royal Portora School, which Oscar Wilde had attended. While reading Modern Languages at Trinity College he lodged in 6 Clare Street, close to Finn Street where Nora Barnacle worked. He represented the college at chess, golf, cricket and even motor racing. He had a difficult relationship with his widowed mother; some say it was why he chose to stay permanently in Paris once he had moved there. He met Joyce there who recognised his talent and encouraged him to write. It wasn't long before Beckett was helping Joyce with his writings, in the role of unpaid secretary. Joyce's daughter, Lucia, fell in love with him and this caused a rift between the two men that lasted for a few years. During this time Beckett wrote stories and poetry. He was not an overnight success and suffered all the angst and doubts, depression and failures of many an aspiring writer. However he became more focused and prolific and produced several books and plays among his post war writings. He is said to have written *Eleutheria* and *Waiting for Godot* in two and four months respectively. When *Godot* was performed he suddenly became a name. In 1969 he was awarded the Nobel Prize for Literature, which he said should have gone to James Joyce. In 1984 he was made a Saoi (Wise One) of Aosdána. He is buried in Montparnasse Cemetery in Paris.

Beckett refers to Dublin in many of his writings – *All that Fall*, *More Pricks than Kicks* and *Dream of Fair to Middling Women*. His works also include *Krapp's Last Tape*, *End Game* and *Malone Dies*. In 2009 Dublin acquired a new, €60million bridge over the river Liffey, an impressive structure representing a harp on its side and designed by the celebrated Spanish architect Santiago Calatrava. It was named the Samuel Beckett Bridge.

Left: A Sunday School prize given to Beckett

Brendan Behan
The Behan Brothers

Brendan, Brian Desmond and Dominic Behan were all products of inner city Dublin and each left his own literary mark in various ways. They lived in a one-room basement flat in the tenement houses in 14 Russell Street.

Brendan, the eldest (1923-64) was born in Holles Street Hospital and went to St Vincent's School in North William Street. He was a Communist and Republican. When convicted of subversive activities in Liverpool he was sentenced to three years in Borstal. Back in Dublin, and following an altercation after the Easter Rising Commemoration in Glasnevin on 5 April 1942 when he was arrested for attempting to shoot a detective, he was given fourteen years hard labour, which was mitigated to four after a general amnesty. He served his sentence between Arbour Hill Prison, the Curragh, County Kildare and Mountjoy Jail. Such sojourns gave him plenty of time to write, along with providing him with copious amounts of material for his plays and a disregard for authority.

He was a well-known figure in the watering holes of Dublin, especially McDaid's pub in Harry Street, and his battle with alcoholism is all too well documented. Coupled with diabetes, it led to his early death. Allegedly, his drinking began when as a small boy his grandmother regularly dispatched him to the local pub for a 'jug o' porter'. He often had a sip or two before giving it to her. He is best remembered for his plays *The Quare Fella*, set in Mountjoy Jail, *Richard's Cork Leg* and *The Hostage*, set in a house on Eccles Street, and for his

autobiography *The Borstal Boy*. When asked by a journalist if there was a message in his plays, he replied, 'what do you think I am – a fecking telegraph pole?'

After his marriage to Beatrice Salkeld in 1954 they lived at 18 Waterloo Road, then at 15 Herbert Street, their last home being 5 Anglesea Road. He is buried in Glasnevin Cemetery in a plot shared with his wife's grandmother Blanaid Salkeld, who was also a writer, and her son Cecil ffrench Salkeld, artist, poet and playwright. Beatrice survived Brendan by twenty-nine years. The couple had two children. Behan's grave remained unmarked for fifteen years. After an article appeared in a national newspaper the local branch of *Conradh na Gaeilge* commissioned a memorial to be erected above it.

He is also commemorated by a wonderful life-size statue showing him relaxing on a bench by the Royal Canal at Dorset Street and Whitworth Road.

Brian Desmond Behan
1926-2002

was born in the Rotunda hospital at a time when the family lived in 14 Russell Street before they moved to Kildare Road, Crumlin. As a youth he was sent to Artane Industrial School for truancy and delinquency. When he had 'reformed' he went to England and later, as a mature student, won a scholarship to Sussex University. His autobiography, *With Breast Expanded*, was followed by a novel, *Time to Go*. He then ghost wrote *Mother of all the Behans*, before turning his mother's life into a novel called *Kathleen, a Dublin Saga*.

Dominic Behan
1928-89

was probably the most prolific of the Behan brothers, but never achieved the fame of his eldest brother. He wrote several plays: *Tell Dublin I*

Miss Her, *The Folk Singer* and *Posterity be Damned*, which was staged in the Gaiety Theatre in 1959. He then went on to write *The Patriot Game*, numerous plays for the BBC for the Armchair Theatre slot and a one man show entitled *Behan being Behan*. He also wrote a novel, many television documentaries and even composed a cantata on the life of Christ. He died in Glasgow and his ashes were scattered on the Royal Canal by his childhood home on Russell Street.

John Betjeman
1906-84

John Betjeman was to become Britain's Poet Laureate, but not until after he had spent several years in Dublin as the Press Attaché in the British Embassy during World War One, with offices at 50 Upper Mount Street. While there he learned Irish and was known to sign his name Seán O'Betejemán! Among his Irish-influenced poems is one he penned called *Ode to the Gaiety Theatre*.

Isaac Bickerstaffe
c.1735-1812

By all accounts a colourful character, this Dublin-born dramatist secured a post as an officer in the Marines, which necessitated a move to London. There he wrote over twenty plays, most of which were produced by playwright, actor and theatre owner David Garrick. Bickerstaffe is credited with writing the script for *Thomas and Sally*, the first comic opera to be staged at Covent Garden, in 1760. With the downsizing of the Marines following the 1763 Treaty of Paris, he was let go and concentrated on his theatrical endeavours in London, many with great success. However, some years later in 1772, to avoid prosecution for alleged homosexuality, he fled to France where he remained and died penniless. *Note: Isaac Bickerstaff was also a pseudonym used by Jonathan Swift.*

Maeve Binchy
1940-

Dalkey-born Maeve Binchy wrote her way into the nation's hearts with her weekly opinion columns as a journalist in *The Irish Times*. She didn't turn to fiction writing until much later, when she claims she was driven by the prospect of unpaid bills to give it a go. She had just returned to Ireland after working in England with writer husband Gordon Snell, a former BBC producer, and had moved into their cottage home in Dalkey, not far from where she grew up. Her first novel,  *Light a Penny Candle*, was published in 1982 and since then she has produced a bestseller every two years, as well as writing countless short stories and talking to thousands of writers and groups. Binchy's debut was to introduce a major protagonist on the Irish woman's fiction scene, a force that inspired many more writers to follow suit. She is known for her generosity and encouragement to writers and for her 'write 1,000 words a day and you'll have your book written in three months' philosophy.

Tara Road made it on to Oprah's Book Club – best novel nominee in 1999 – the same year that she was given a Lifetime Achievement Award at the Nibbles (British Book Awards). *Tara Road* has since been made into a film, so too have *Echoes*, *How About You* and *Circle of Friends*, which starred Minnie Driver and Chris O'Donnell.

Maeve Binchy and her husband still live in the cottage in Dalkey where they both sit at the desks in the same room and write.

Snell is the author of many well-loved children's books including *The Phantom Horsemen*, *Lottie's Lette*, *Amy's Wonderful Nest* and *Tina and the Tooth Fairy*. He was a regular scriptwriter for the long-running children's series 'Wanderly Wagon' on RTÉ.

Sara Berkeley
1967-

Poet Sara Berkeley was born in Dublin in 1967 and now lives in California. Her works appear in many collections including *The Picador Book of Contemporary Irish Fiction* and *The Penguin Book of Contemporary Irish Poetry*.

Eavan Boland
1944-

Poet Eavan Boland was born in Dublin but as the child of a diplomat father she lived abroad for much of her youth, only to return at fourteen. She attended the Holy Child School in Killiney and then Trinity College. She published her first volume shortly afterwards, *New Territory*. She wrote *W.B. Yeats and His World* with Micheál MacLiammóir. In subsequent works she explored a great diversity of topics: the ordinary lives of women, aggression, nationhood and suburbia. *Night Feed*, *Against Love Poetry* and more recently *The Lost*

Land and *Domestic Violence* offer a comprehensive spectrum. She is married to writer Kevin Casey and they live in Dundrum.

Dermot Bolger
1959-

Poet, playwright, novelist and publisher Dermot Bolger is an impressive force in the publishing scene in Dublin. He was educated at St Canice's National School and then at Beneavin De La Salle College in Finglas. At just eighteen he set up the Raven Arts Press, releasing debut poetry collections and books by many well known names on the literary circuit. In 1992 he became involved in co-founding a new publishing house, New Island. He has written nine novels, including *The Valparaiso Voyage*, *The Family on Paradise Pier* and a crossover novel for young adults, *New Town Soul*. His plays *The Ballymun Trilogy* capture the birth, demolition and the regeneration of a very real high rise satellite town, revealing the hidden lives therein. He adapted Joyce's *Ulysses* for the stage under the title *A Dublin Bloom*, and edited the poetry anthology *Night and Day – Twenty Four Hours in the Life of Dublin*.

Bolger also devised the very popular best-selling collaborative novels, *Finbar's Hotel* and *Ladies Night at Finbar's Hotel*, with chapters written by seven different leading Irish writers, but leaving the reader to guess who wrote which chapter.

His numerous awards include the Samuel Beckett Award 1990, Æ Memorial Award 1996 and The Stuart Parker BBC Award 1990. He is also a member of Aosdána.

Dion Boucicault
c1820-90

Born at 47 Lower Gardiner Street, a very fashionable residence of its time, Dionysius Lardner Boursiquot, later Dion Boucicault, spent his early years here. He began writing dramatic sketches and took up acting under the stage

Photo: Getty Images

name of Lee Moreton. His first major production was *London Assurance* at Covent Garden which opened the doors for twenty-two of his plays being produced on the London stage within the next four years. He married a French wife and moved to France, but the lady died in mysterious circumstances and he returned to England where he lived far beyond his means and soon found himself in debt. He recovered some of his reputation with *The Corsican Brothers* but decided to move to New York with his new wife, and was soon a hit there with plays like *The Poor of New York*, *Dot* and *The Octoroon*, tackling issues such as urban poverty and slavery. His last New York play was *The Colleen Bawn*, which he took to the London stage where it ran for 247 performances at the Adelphi Theatre. He wrote several more successful plays, including *The Shaughran* and *Robert Emmet*. In 1885 he took off for New Zealand, where he married again, without divorcing his second wife! Although he lived abroad for most of his life, when asked if he was an Irishman he replied, 'Nature gave me that honour.'

He returned to Dublin many times and staged his *Arrah-na-Pogue* play at the Theatre Royal in Hawkins Street. He took a starring role as Conn in *The Shaughraun* in 1874. It is reported that when this play moved to New York the following year it netted him half a million dollars, which he squandered. He was, however, instrumental in getting the 1856 Copyright Laws passed by Congress before that. He is buried in Mount Hope Cemetery, Saw Mills Road, Hastings on Hudson, New York.

Elizabeth Bowen
1899-1973

Elizabeth Bowen was a very productive novelist and short story writer who was born at 15 Herbert Place, Dublin. Although the family home was an impressive pile, Bowen's Court in County Cork, she spent a lot of her time in this house, particularly during wintertime, which she recreates so vividly in her book, *Seven Winters, Memories of a Dublin Childhood*. Through her eyes we relive a childhood of privilege, dancing classes, genteel strolls along tree-lined 'red roads' – her description for the Georgian avenues and squares with their red-bricked houses. (This was published by The Cuala Press, 1942, a private publishing house set up by Elizabeth (Lolly) Yeats, sister of WB Yeats, to print works of the Celtic Revival). In another book, *The Shelbourne*, Elizabeth Bowen gives wonderfully

The Smithwick brewing family from Kilkenny leaving the Shelbourne Hotel. (photo courtesy of the Shelbourne Hotel)

descriptive images of Dublin society. As an adult she used to stay in the hotel, among the celebrities and guests who had come to town to do 'the season' and attend soirees and regimental balls. Prospective marriages were brokered or tabooed and diaries filled with dressmaking appointments and visits to the fashionable milliners in the vicinity of the hotel. She also enjoyed outings to Bewleys Oriental Café in Grafton Street.

Bowen went on to write over twenty books. She was awarded an honorary degree of Doctor of Letters from Trinity College. She is buried with her husband, Alan Charles Cameron, at Farahy Churchyard, County Cork, close to where Bowen's Court used to stand.

Clare Boylan
1948-2006

Dublin-born and convent educated at St Louis High School, Rathmines, Clare Boylan worked as a journalist and magazine editor before becoming a full time writer. A self-confessed feminist, her first novel *Holy Pictures* is set in 1920s Dublin and written from the perspective of a typically indoctrinated Catholic teenager of the time, observing her parents' dismal marriage. Boylan put marriage under the spotlight again in her *Beloved Strangers*, when illness separates a couple that have been together for fifty years. Boylan wrote six novels and several collections of short stories. The film *Making Waves*, was based on one of these – *Some Ladies on a Tour* – and was nominated for an Oscar in 1988.

She also wrote *Emma Brown* as a continuation of a two-chapter unfinished work by Charlotte Brontë. She lived in County Wicklow.

John Boyne
1971-

Dubliner John Boyne came to international notice with his novel, *The Boy in the Striped Pyjamas*, a story about the Holocaust. It was made into an award-winning Miramax film, spent more than 80 weeks at no.1 in Ireland, topped the *New York Times* bestseller list, and was the bestselling book in Spain in both 2007 and 2008. Worldwide, it has sold more than 5 million copies and has been translated into more than 40 languages. He is reputed to have written the first draft in two and a half days, hardly sleeping at all. No doubt his late night writing session after his lectures at Trinity and his job in booksellers Waterstones gave him plenty of practise in coping with sleep deprivation. Among his many awards are: Irish Book Awards – People's Choice Book of the Year, Irish Book Awards – Children's Book of the Year, Bisto Children's Book of the Year (2007); The Qué Leer Award for Best International Novel of the Year, Spain (in translation), 2008; Orange Prize Readers Group Book of the Year, 2009. Other works include *Next of Kin*, *The House of Special Purpose*, and *Norah Barleywater Runs Away*.

WHAT DUBLIN MEANS TO ME ... JOHN BOYNE

It's the history. It's the love of words. It's Joyce in his tower and Wilde in Merrion Square. It's the walls of the Duke, decorated with the faces of thirsty dead writers, staring at us as we sink one more before the Nitelink takes us home. It's Davy Byrne's on Bloomsday. It's the bookshops on Dawson Street, the students reading second-hand novels in Fellows' Square. It's the New Writing pages in the *Tribune*, the literary supplement in *The Irish Times*. It's the Edmund Burke theatre at Trinity College, visiting writers reading short stories to an audience gathered on the stairs. It's seeing ol' Pat outside the Bank of Ireland on College Green, selling his poems for whatever you'll give him. It's the buskers singing *One* on Grafton Street while travelling children screech about what happened by lonely prison walls. It's a city of literature, of course it is. It's Dublin.

Maeve Brennan
1917-93

A colourful character on the US literary scene, Maeve Brennan was born in Great Denmark Street, Dublin while her father, Robert, was imprisoned for his part in the 1916 Rising. He had been sentenced to death but that was commuted to a term of detention. The family moved to Ranelagh and then to Washington when Robert was appointed as the Irish Free State's first minister to the United States. The Dalkey-born editor of *Harper's Bazaar*, Carmel Snow, soon noticed her writings. She hired her services and, before long, *The New Yorker* poached her where she became popular as 'The Long-Winded Lady'. Despite spending the rest of her life in the States she frequently used her childhood home in Dublin as the backdrop for over half of her forty plus short stories. She is the aunt of novelist and playwright Roddy Doyle (*see p45*).

Henry Brooke
1703-83

Henry Brooke was a clergyman's son who was educated at Sheridan's Academy in Capel Street, (owned and run by Richard Brinsley Sheridan's grandfather) and later at Trinity College. He moved to London to study law but came home prematurely when his aunt died. She had appointed him as guardian of her twelve-year old daughter. He married her when she was fourteen and he just twenty. They had twenty-two children together, of whom only two survived them. His Dublin address was on South William Street. He wrote *The Earl of Westmoreland* and other works specifically for the Dublin theatres. A legacy in 1764 left him financially comfortable and able to concentrate on his writings and build a home in Cavan, where he was born. Two year later he published the first of five volumes of his greatest work, *The Fool of Quality*, a work he didn't complete until 1770. His contemporary John Wesley pronounced it 'one of the most beautiful pictures that ever was drawn in the world; the strokes are so delicately fine, the touches so easy, natural, and affecting, that I know not who can survey it with tearless eyes, unless he has a heart of stone.'

Christy Brown
1932-81

Christy Brown was born in the Rotunda Hospital, one of twenty-two children. He grew up in Stanaway Road, Crumlin, where he spent a childhood coping with the constraints of severe cerebral palsy. His mother taught him the alphabet and, holding chalk and a paintbrush with his toes, he began to write and paint. With the help of his brothers, who typed his notes, and the encouragement of his physician Doctor Robert Collis, himself a playwright, he began composing his autobiography *My Left Foot*. This gave a rich insight into his life and challenges as well as a compelling portrait of working class Dublin in the 40s and 50s. Fellow Dubliner Jim Sheridan filmed the book after his death. It won an Academy Award for Daniel Day Lewis who played the role of Christy. Brown left behind several books including *Down All the Days*, which the Irish rock band The Pogues commemorated in a track on one of their albums. He also published three poetry collections. Brown's last book, *A Promising Career*, was published posthumously. He met Mary Carr, his future wife, in London and they married in the Registry Office in Kildare Street, Dublin where he signed the register with his left foot. They subsequently lived in Rathcoole, County Dublin, before moving to Kerry and then to England, where he died. He is buried in a family plot in Glasnevin Cemetery. A stone inscribed with the title of one of his poems, '*Come Softly to My Wake*' was added some time after his death.

Edmund Burke
1730-97

Dublin-born Edmund Burke is one of the few literati to be commemorated by a statue outside the hallowed halls of Trinity College and to have a campus theatre named after him. While a student there in 1747, he set up a debating club, which was known as Edmund Burke's Club. A few years afterwards it merged with the Historical Club to form the College Historical Society. It's better known today as 'The Hist' and is reputed to be the oldest undergraduate society of its kind in the world. Some of the minutes from those early meetings have survived. He is remembered as a poet, an orator, a politician, philosopher and historian, as well as for his role in speaking out in support of free trade with Ireland and Catholic emancipation – issues which lost him his seat in the House of Commons. He also supported the American Civil War and denounced the French Revolution. His bronze monument in the front grounds of Trinity College was unveiled in 1868 by the Prince of Wales while visiting Dublin (*see photo opposite*).

'People will not look forward to

posterity, who never look backward to their ancestors.' –from Burke's *Reflections on the Revolution of France*.

William Carleton
1794-1869

William Carleton was a novelist and storyteller whose *Traits and Stories of the Irish Peasantry* tell a very vivid story of life before the great famine in Ireland. A native of Clogher, County Tyrone, he was educated at some of the 'hedge schools' which remained a source of education even after the Penal Laws, which had forbidden Catholic schools, were repealed in 1782. In sheds and mud huts and under hedges, students became proficient in the basics, along with Greek and Latin. He walked to Dublin and there made a precarious living from his writings, contributing regularly to the *Dublin University Magazine* and to *The Nation*. In his autobiography he recalls how he was forced to sleep in a basement one night when he found himself penniless.

He left some good chronicles of life in pre and post famine Ireland, of landlordism and poverty, both in *Traits and Stories of Irish Peasantry* and *The Black Prophet – A Tale of Irish Famine*. He is buried in Mount Jerome Cemetery (*see monument below*). Carleton is commemorated with the annual Carleton Summer School in Clogher Valley, County Tyrone.

Marina Carr
1964-

Marina Carr came to Dublin from County Offaly to attend UCD, where she wrote her first play *Ullaloo*. However, her second play, *Low in the Dark*, was staged two years before *Ullaloo* got its first airing. Her background was literary – her mother wrote poetry in Irish, and her father, Hugh, had plays staged at the Abbey, Peacock and Gate Theatres. As well as writing numerous plays, Marina has served as writer-in-residence at the Abbey Theatre and Trinity College. In February 2009 she debuted two plays in Dublin – *Marble* at the Abbey – and a children's play, *The Giant Blue Hand*, at The Ark. (Dublin's Cultural Centre for Children).

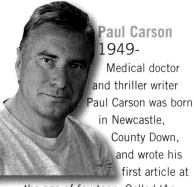

Paul Carson
1949-

Medical doctor and thriller writer Paul Carson was born in Newcastle, County Down, and wrote his first article at the age of fourteen. Called 'An evening at the Abbey Theatre' it appeared in his college magazine. After studying medicine at Trinity College and spending some years in Australia, he came back to Ireland in 1984 to develop his own medical practice in Stillorgan, County Dublin. He began writing health books, then children's books and finally he turned to thrillers with great success. *Scalpel* was followed by *Cold Steel*, *Final Duty*, *Ambush* and *Betrayal*.

Elizabeth Casey
c1845-94

Novelist Elizabeth Casey (who wrote under the name E. Owens Blackburne) was blind as a child, but had her sight restored by Oscar Wilde's father, Sir William Wilde. She began writing for a Dublin humorous publication, *Zozimus*, which was called after the blind balladeer, Michael Moran, who bore this nickname.

She later moved to London where she wrote some twenty novels, many of them with a feminist slant, including *A Woman Scorned*, *The Way Women Love*, as well as the two volumes of biography, *Illustrious Irish Women*. She returned to Ireland to be close to her mother, who lived in Fairview. She met a tragic end when she tried to rescue her mother from a fire that had started in her mother's room. Elizabeth was to die a few days later from her burns. Her mother survived.

Seamus Cashman
1943-

The County Cork-born publisher, poet and editor has lived and worked in Dublin for most of his adult life. He established Wolfhound Press in1974 as a literary and cultural publishing house and was its publisher for 27 years. He has written three poetry collections: *That Morning Will Come*, *Carnival*, and *Clowns and Acrobats* amongst other works. He is a Board Member of Children's Books Ireland.

Austin Clarke
1896-1974

Austin Clarke was born in 83 Manor Street, but his family moved to 15 Mountjoy Square when he was three. His autobiographical account *Twice Round the Black Church* takes readers back to a childhood in Edwardian times. He attended the long gone Christian Brothers School in St Mary's Place and went to Mass with his family in Berkeley Road. He cycled down to O'Connell Street (then Sackville Street) immediately after the Rising in 1916, to see the new green white and orange flag of the Republic being shown for the first time as it fluttered over the General Post Office.

Clarke was an accomplished musician as well as one of Ireland's most successful poets. He spent seventeen years working in England and produced over thirty works of poetry, fiction (all of which was banned by the Irish Censorship Board), drama and two volumes of autobiography. He studied under Thomas MacDonagh and Douglas Hyde in UCD and later replaced MacDonagh as a lecturer there. He was forced to forfeit this position when he married in a registry office. The marriage didn't last and he moved to England. He remarried and on his return he settled in Bridge House, Templeogue. In one of his poems he talks about the moment he realised the city was encroaching on his bucolic idyll, on hearing some new church bells ringing about a mile away. Bridge House has since been demolished, as has the bridge. However, the new bridge at Templeogue was named after the poet.

As well as having a weekly poetry programme on national radio, Clarke started the Dublin Verse Speaking Society, originally based in the Peacock Theatre. After three years it relocated to the Abbey Theatre under its own name, The Lyric Theatre, where it thrived until 1951 when the Abbey was destroyed by fire.

His legacy to the nation is his personal library of over 5,000 works of poetry, prose, drama, literary criticism and biography, which now form a large part of the Poetry Ireland Library, housed in the UCD Library Special Collections at Belfield.

Above: Clarke plaque in the Literary Parade in St Patrick's Park

Brian Coffey
1905-95

Dun Laoghaire-born Brian Coffey was one of the Irish Modernist poets to emerge in the 1920s. His first collection, *Poems*, was a joint publication with Denis Devlin in 1930. Samuel Beckett's reaction to it was to describe them as 'without question the most interesting of the youngest generation of Irish poets.' Coffey's later works include *Advent*, *Chanterelles: Short Poems*, *Poems and Versions* and *Poems from Mallarmé*.

Padraic Colum
1881-1972

Born Patrick Collumn, playwright, poet and novelist Padraic Colum grew up in Glasthule where his father was the stationmaster at Sandycove. He changed his name to the Irish spelling when he joined the Irish League and came in contact with James Joyce, WB Yeats and Arthur Griffith. He lived at several addresses in the Donnybrook area: 2 Belmont Avenue and Bushville Terrace, off Marlborough Road. His last address was close by at 11 Edenvale Road. He got his first real break when *The Land* was staged at Abbey Theatre. He then concentrated for a time on writing poetry. With a move to the United States with his suffragette wife he began writing successful children's books, flavoured with his love of his homeland. *A Boy in Eireann* and *The King of Ireland's Son* were two favourites at the time and any adult of a certain vintage in Ireland today will recall learning his poem *An Old Woman of the Roads*. By the end of his life Colum's literary legacy included numerous novels, epic poems, plays and poetry. He died in Connecticut and his body was brought home to be buried, beside his wife, Mary, in St Fintan's Cemetery, Sutton. Their grave is marked with a traditional Celtic Cross with an inscription by his friend, AE. It says simply: *'The Giant has come back to his mountain.'*

Marita Conlon-McKenna
1956-

Marita Conlon-McKenna is one of Ireland's most successful children's writers as well as being the author of popular adult fiction titles. She grew up in Goatstown and lives in south Dublin. A past pupil of Mount Anville School, she made her name with a children's book, *Under the Hawthorn Tree*, which she wrote after hearing a radio report of the finding of an unmarked grave from the Famine period. It was the first in her Children of the Famine trilogy, followed by *Wildflower Girl* and *Fields of Home*. The books have become classics and have been translated into many languages. Marita has won several awards, including the International Reading Association Award, the Osterreichischer Kinder und Jugendbuchpreis, the Reading Association of Ireland Award and the Bisto Book of the Year Award. Among her adult fiction titles are *The Stone House*, *The Hat Shop on the Corner*, *Mother of the Bride* and *School for Cooks*.

> MY DUBLIN –
> MARITA CONLON-MCKENNA
> Dublin, my city – your streets burst with life and energy and your big old heart is full of stories – it's no wonder you are a city of writers.

John Connolly
1968-

Dubliner John Connolly studied English at Trinity College and journalism in Dublin City University. He spent several years freelancing before he invented the character of Charlie Parker, a former policeman who is hunting the killer of his wife and daughter. Parker first appeared in *Every Dead Thing* (1999). Since then there have been nine successful Charlie Parker novels, as well as a stand alone book, a novella and several short stories. Other titles include *The Black Angel*, *The Book of Lost Things* and *The Whisperers*. He has won numerous awards including the Hughes and Hughes Book of the Year for *The Book of Lost Things*. *The New Daughter* is a film adaptation of his short story *Nocturnes* and stars Kevin Kostner.

June Considine
1945-

Malahide-based Considine has published for both adults and children. Her books for young readers include *The Luvender Trilogy*, *View from a Blind Bridge*, *The Glass Triangle*, and the Beachwood series for young adults. Her adult novels include *Deceptions* and *When the Bough Breaks*. Her last two, *The Prodigal Sister* and *Stolen Child* have been written under the pseudonym Laura Elliott. Considine is a sister of Dermot Bolger (*see p25*).

Tim Pat Coogan
1935-

Timothy Patrick Coogan wears many hats – he is a historian, a biographer and a former newspaper editor. His childhood home was at Tudor Hall in Monkstown, County Dublin. He went to the local Christian Brothers School in Dun Laoghaire before moving on to Belvedere and Blackrock Colleges. He became the editor of the *Irish Press* – a tenure he held from 1968 until 1987. Since then he has written several critically acclaimed books on modern Irish history, and a memoir. His books include *The IRA*, *Ireland Since the Rising*, *On the Blanket – the H-block Story*, *Wherever Green is Worn*, *The Troubles*, *1916*, as well as controversial biographies of *Éamon de Valera* and *Michael Collins*.

His mother, Beatrice Coogan, was a writer and an actress who played at the Abbey Theatre. She is best remembered for her book *The Big Wind*, which won the Frankfurt Book Fair Book of the Year 1969.

Anthony Cronin
1928-

Wexford-born but Dublin-based Anthony Cronin is a celebrated poet. Among his many achievements is the Marten Toonder Award he received in 1983 for his contribution to Irish literature. In 2003 he was elevated to the rank of Saoi in Aosdána. As well as numerous volumes of poetry he also penned a biography of Samuel Beckett. His collections include *RMS Titanic*, *The End of the Modern World* and *Relationships*. Cronin was cultural advisor to then Taoiseach Charles Haughey when the special tax regime which enables artists and writers resident in Ireland to avail of exemptions on income from their creative work was introduced.

Conor Cruise O'Brien
1917-2008

Politician, scholar, writer, journalist and historian, Conor Cruise O'Brien, who was educated at Sandford Park, D6, was nothing if not controversial. Among his works is *The Great Melody: A Thematic Biography of Edmund Burke*. His autobiography, *Memoir: My Life and Themes*, shows the many aspects of the man and his interests, and his collection of essays, *Cunning and Passion*, includes a substantial piece on the literary work of William Butler Yeats, but perhaps his most contentious work is *The Siege*, written in 1989. This offers a sympathetic history of Zionism and the State of Israel.

Kate Cruise O'Brien
1948-98

was educated at Rathgar Junior School, Park House, Rathfarnham, and then at TCD. By the age of twenty-two she had won the Hennessy Literary Award and her collection of short stories, *A Gift Horse*, won the Rooney Prize for Irish Literature. She also wrote *The Homesick Garden*. She became a literary editor with Poolbeg Press, discovering and fostering much of the new writing talent that emerged in the late 1980s and 90s. She lived in Ranelagh and died suddenly, aged 50.

Thomas Davis
1814-45

Nationalist, poet, writer and co-founder of the weekly newspaper, *The Nation*, Thomas Davis was born in County Cork, but the family moved to Dublin, and, after living at Warrington Place by the Grand Canal, they later settled at 67 Lower Baggot Street. There he died at the very early age of thirty. It is reported that the cause was scarlet fever or tuberculosis, both incurable diseases at the time. He achieved much in his short life: graduating from Trinity with a law degree, he became joint editor of *The Morning Register* with John Blake Dillon, and they went on to become founders of *The Nation* in 1942, along with Charles Gavan Duffy. This gave Davis a platform for his nationalist views and the paper is often credited with being the precursor of the Celtic Literary Revival. It survived him and published regularly until 1891. The offices were located in Middle Abbey Street, in a building that subsequently became home to the *Irish Independent*, *Sunday Independent* and *Evening Herald* newspapers. A wall plaque commemorates *The Nation* on Independent House, although Independent Newspapers moved out some years ago. Davis is remembered for his nationalist writings and for his ballads and songs, many patriotic in nature. Perhaps one of his best known is *A Nation Once Again*, with its rousing chorus:

A Nation once again,
A Nation once again,
And Ireland, long a province, be
A Nation once again!

Statue of Thomas Davis on College Green

CYPHERS

Cyphers Magazine began publishing prose, poetry and art in 1975 and has continued ever since, with the aid of the Arts Council. Its four founders were: **Eiléan Ní Chuilleanáin**, **Macdara Woods**, **Leland Bardwell** and **Pearse Hutchinson** – all now members of Aosdána.

Eiléan Ní Chuilleanáin
1942-

The Cork-born poet, a daughter of Eilís Dillon, began lecturing in Trinity College around the same time that she won the Irish Times Poetry Award in 1966. Her first collection, *Acts and Monuments*, was published in 1972. This was followed by many more, *The Girl Who Married the Reindeer*, *The Magdalene Sermon* and *The Rose Geranium* among them.

Macdara Woods
1942-

A Dubliner who was educated at Gonzaga College, D6, he later married Eiléan Ní Chuilleanáin. His works span sixteen collections of poetry, including *The Sixteenth Kind of Fear* and *Seconds Out*.

Leland Bardwell
1928-

Leland Bardwell was born in India, but educated in Dublin and London. She has published numerous novels and books of poetry as well as a memoir entitled *A Restless Life*.

Pearse Hutchinson
1927-

Born in Glasgow of Irish parents, poet Pearse Hutchinson was educated by the Christian Brothers at Synge Street and UCD. His first collection was *Tongue without Hands*; his latest *At Least for a While*.

Poetry
Joseph Allen, Leland Bardwell
Juana Bignozzi *(translation)*
Kieran Furey, Ndrek Gjini
Richard W. Halperin, James Harpur
Simon Jackson, Teresa Lally, Leo Lavery
Naton Leslie, Brian Leyden, Tom MacIntyre
Nicholas McLachlan, Patrick Maddock
Patrick Moran, Caitriona Ní Chleirchín
Patricia O'Callaghan, Ger Reidy,
Tadhg Russell, Janet Shepperson,
Donna Sørensen, Richard Tillinghast
Robert Anthony Welch, Macdara Woods
Vincent Woods, Howard Wright

Fiction
Liam Aungier
Lucy E.M. Black, Rita Jacob

Parables of Franciscan complexity
Seán Hutton

Two etchings
Brian Lalor

71

Two statues commemorate Davis in Dublin: one over his grave in Mount Jerome Cemetery, Harold's Cross, and one on College Green, erected in 1977 (*see p39*).

Gerald Dawe
1952-

Belfast-born writer and poet Gerald Dawe lived in Galway for many years before moving to Dublin where he has lived since the late 1980s. He is a fellow of Trinity College and a director of the Oscar Wilde Centre for Irish Writing. His poetry collections include *Sunday School*, *The Morning Train*, *Lake Geneva* and *Points West*. *The World as Province: Selected Prose* was published in 2010

John F Deane
1943-

Poet, novelist and publisher John F Deane was born on Achill Island in the west of Ireland. He was instrumental in setting up *Poetry Ireland* and *Poetry Ireland Review*. He was also the founder and editor of Dedalus Press. His work is widely recognised and in 1996 he was elected as Secretary General of the

European Academy of Poetry. His poetry collections include *The Instruments of Art* and *A Little Book of Hours*. He wrote two novels, *In the Name of the Wild* and *Undertow*. He is a member of Aosdána.

Eilís Dillon
1920-94

Eilís Dillon was a native of Galway, but lived in Dublin for many years, where she fought tirelessly for the arts and was active in a number of public and cultural bodies. She served on the Arts Council, the International Commission for English in the Liturgy, the Irish Writers' Union and the Irish Writers' Centre. She was a Fellow of the Royal Society of Literature, and a member of Aosdána. In between bringing up three children and running a student hostel for the university, she developed her writing into a highly successful professional career, producing children's books in Irish and English, then started to write novels and detective stories. The Eilís Dillon Award is a special prize given annually as part of the Bisto Book Awards to a new or emerging writer. She herself had won the main Bisto Book of the Year award in 1989 with *The Island of Ghosts*. She was the mother of poet Eiléan Ní Chuilleanáin (*see p40*)

Patrick Dinneen
1860-1934

Patrick Dinneen, or Pádraig Ua Duinnín, was an Irish lexicographer and historian from Kerry. He joined the Society of Jesus in 1880 and was ordained a priest in 1894, but resigned the order six years later to devote his life to the study of the Irish language. He was a leading figure in the Irish Texts Society. He also wrote a novel and a play in Irish, and translated such works as Charles Dickens's *A Christmas Carol* into Irish. His best-known work, however, is his Irish-English dictionary, *Foclóir Gaedhilge agus Béarla*, first published in 1904. All the plates for this were destroyed by fire in the 1916 Rising. In 1934 he collapsed on the steps of the National Library, where he was a frequent visitor, and died shortly afterwards. He is buried in Glasnevin Cemetery.

Excerpt from *No Goodbye* by Marita Conlon-McKenna
(The O'Brien Press 1994)

The Picnic

The car climbs the winding roads through the leafy spring countryside, up into the Dublin Mountains. Then we go higher up on foot, up steep forest mountain paths. We're all panting. Still, I love the smell of pine needles, and the soft crunch of them under your feet as you walk, and the dull thump as you push your way through the moss and ferns.

'Come on! Keep going!' Dad yells at us.

He leads the way and we follow him like a scout troop. No matter what way you look, all you can see is trees and more trees. The further we march, the further away home seems to be. Suddenly I can spot snatches of blue and glimmers of yellow-gold, one patch, then another, as sunlight dazzles through the trees at the end of the path.

'Top of the world!' shouts Grace.

And do you know, she's right. When I look downwards the land seems to tilt and almost makes me dizzy. Dublin is spread out in the distance – factories, offices and high church steeples, all like a little toy town. The River Liffey meanders like a shiny, blue-grey snail trail through the places we know and love, down to the docks, then out into the vast blue brightness of Dublin Bay. Conor says he can see our road, and Grace says she can see our house!

JP Donleavy
1926-

James Patrick Donleavy was born in New York of Irish parents. After completing a tour of duty with the US Navy during WWII he moved to Dublin to study at Trinity College. He never got his degree, but was a well known figure in the local pubs and had his first writings published in the Dublin literary periodical *Envoy*. He wrote many novels and plays but is best remembered for his novel *The Ginger Man*, and his nonfiction work *JP Donleavy's Ireland*.

A pub in Fenian Street now bears the name The Ginger Man. Donleavy's preferred drinking establishments were The Bailey on Duke Street and Mc Daids. The former is where he is reputed to have allowed Brendan Behan read some of his work in progress, even permitting him to scribble some suggestions in the margins of his manuscript – suggestions which made it into the final drafts. The book was banned for obscenity both in Ireland and in USA. Later the story was adapted for stage and famously enjoyed a three-show run at the Gaiety Theatre, before being axed when pressure was brought to bear by the Catholic hierarchy. A wake was held in The Bailey, attended by actor Richard Harris, who had played the lead, Sebastian Dangerfield. The character of Dangerfield is said to be based on a McDaid's regular, Gainor Christ.

Not one to bear a grudge, Donleavy later moved to Ireland and took up Irish citizenship.

BANNED IN IRELAND
Over the years countless books were banned in Ireland in a effort to protect its citizens from exposure to topics that were deemed by the guardians of our morality as unsuitable, explicit, inflammatory, politically subversive or just because they were considered downright immoral! Although 'the ban' was never formally rescinded, gradually all of the titles were reinstated.

At least three of Benedict Kiely's books were banned, prompting the comment from him on his eightieth birthday: 'If you weren't banned it meant you were no bloody good!'

Brendan Behan's *Borstal Boy* is believed to have been banned for its views on Irish republicanism and the Catholic Church as well as for its depiction of adolescent sexuality.

Edna O'Brien's *The Country*

Girls got on the list in 1960 for its explicit sexual content. *The Lonely Girl* was banned two years later after Archbishop John Charles McQuaid personally complained to the then Minister for Justice, Charles Haughey, saying that this book was 'particularly bad'.

Maura Laverty's second novel *Alone We Embark*, published in the US as *Touched by the Thorn*, won the Irish Women Writers Award in 1943, but it had been banned the previous year for its immoral content – its married heroine was unfaithful.

Lee Dunne's *Paddy Maguire is Dead* was banned here in 1972 while it was openly on sale in the UK.

Other writers and their works that were censored include *The House of Gold* by Liam O'Flaherty, *The Adventures of the Black Girl in Search of her God* by George Bernard Shaw, *Windfalls* by Sean O'Casey, *Watt* by Samuel Beckett and *Midsummer Night Madness* by Sean O Faoláin.

Contrary to popular belief, *Ulysses* was never banned in Ireland, although it was banned in the US where it was serialised, and in the UK.

Emma Donoghue
1969-

Dubliner Emma Donoghue attended UCD before moving to England to take a PhD in Cambridge University on the concept of friendship between men and women in eighteenth-century English fiction. She started making her living from writing at twenty-three and hasn't stopped since. She now lives in Canada. She has written drama for stage and radio and her numerous novels include *The Sealed Letter*, *Masked*, *The Woman Who Gave Birth to Rabbits* and *Room*, which was shortlisted for the Man Booker Prize in 2010. It also won the Rogers Trust Fiction Prize and the Irish Book Award 2010.

Katie Donovan
1962-

Wexford-born poet Katie Donovan studied at Trinity College Dublin and at the University of California at Berkeley before moving back to Dublin where she worked as a journalist with *The Irish Times*. She is an Amatsu practitioner (a form of Japanese osteopathy) and combines this work with writing poetry and part-time lecturing in Creative Writing at IADT, Dun Laoghaire, where she now lives. Her collections include *Watermelon Man*, *Entering the Mare*, *Day of the Dead* and *Rootling: New and Selected Poems*.

Theo Dorgan
1953-

Cork-born Theo Dorgan now lives in Dublin. He began publishing his poetry when he was still an undergraduate, studying under poet John Montague. His collections include *The Ordinary House of Love*, *Rosa Mundi* and *Sappho's Daughter*.

Dorgan is well known for his work as a radio and television broadcaster and for being a director of Poetry Ireland, the national poetry organisation.

Roddy Doyle
1958-

Roddy Doyle grew up in Kilbarrack, County Dublin and was educated by the Christian Brothers at St Fintan's School in Sutton before going on to UCD. He taught English and Geography for fourteen years at Greendale Community School in Kilbarrack. During his career in the classroom he no doubt got plenty of material for some of his subsequent books and characters. His first novel, *The Commitments*, was made into a very successful movie in 1991, directed by Alan Parker. It became part of the Barrytown Trilogy – the other two books being *The Snapper* and *The Van*. *The Van* was shortlisted for the Booker Prize in 1991.

Two years later *Paddy Clarke Ha Ha Ha* won that coveted award and it was that which prompted Doyle to give up teaching and write full time. His next book *The Woman who Walked into Doors* introduced us to Paula Spencer, whom we meet again ten years later in her own right as *Paula Spencer*. Doyle has written numerous short stories, a book about his parents, *Rory and Ita*, screenplays, plays for theatre and children's books. He now lives in Killiney.

MY DUBLIN – RODDY DOYLE
What does Dublin mean to me? It's very simple: No Dublin, no Doyle.

Excerpt from *The Deportees* by Roddy Doyle (Vintage, 2007)

I Understand

I walk. Through Temple Bar. Along the river, past tourists and heroin addicts, strangely sitting together. Past the Halfpenny Bridge and O'Connell Bridge. Past the Custom House and the statues of the starving Irish people. I walk to the Point Depot. Across the bridge – the rain has stopped, the clouds are low – I walk past the tollbooths, to Sandymount. No cars slow down, no car door slams behind me. I am alone.

I walk on the wet sand. I see men in the distance, digging holes in the sand. They dig for worms, I think. They look as if they stand on the sea. It is very beautiful here. The ocean, the low mountains, the wind.

It is becoming dark when I cross the tracks at the station called Sydney Parade.

I will go to work. I will not let them stop me. I will go to work. I will buy a bicycle. I will buy a mobile phone. I am staying. I will not paint myself blue. I will not disappear.

It is dark now. It is dangerous. Cars approach, and pass.

I walk the distance to Temple Bar. I walk through crowds and along parts of the streets that are empty. I pass men alone and women in laughing groups.

FIGHTING WORDS
In 2009 Roddy Doyle, along with Sean Love, established a creative writing centre in Behan Square off Russell Street, Dublin1 where Brendan Behan and his brothers used to live. This venture is called Fighting Words and was inspired by 826 Valencia in San Francisco – a project aimed not only at getting schoolchildren excited about writing, but to provide stimulation and encouragement to teachers too. However it's not confined to the classroom, but targeted to help students of all ages to develop and love their writing skill. There is no age limit and all tutoring is given free.
www.fightingwords.ie

Lee Dunne
1934-

Lee Dunne was born in Mount Pleasant Buildings in Rathmines and attended St Mary's National School and then Tranquilla School before leaving at 14 with just a Primary Certificate. After various jobs in Dublin he emigrated to England to make a living. He spent a year riding a bicycle around London doing 'The Knowledge' in order to become a cabbie so that he would have more time to write. He claims he wrote his first four books in a week each and when his fifth took thirteen days he thought he was losing his touch!

Dunne came to prominence in 1965 with his novel *Goodbye to the Hill*, followed by the other parts of this trilogy – *A Bed in the Sticks* and *Paddy Maguire is Dead*. His first eight books were banned, as were the two films for which he wrote the screenplays. These were *Paddy*, based on *Goodbye to the Hill* and *Wedding Night*. He went on to become a prolific writer, with 18 novels, 10 stage plays and two Hollywood productions to his name, along with a plethora of radio and television plays and over 2,000 episodes of radio scripts for *Harbour Hotel*, *Konvenience Korner*, *Callan*, *Troubleshooters*, *Fair City* and *The Kennedys of Castleross*. His memoir, *My Middle Name is Lucky*, recalls the waves of fortune that never quite managed to swamp his ebullient spirit. He lives in Greystones, County Wicklow with his wife, Maura.

MY DUBLIN – LEE DUNNE
I used to deliver milk in my bare feet to the posh houses in Rathgar. Only a mile divided our neighbourhoods, but it could have been a different continent. They had flowers and trees and grass; there were seven of us in two rooms and the family who lived above us had eighteen children in the same space.

Paul Durcan
1944-

Poet Paul Durcan was born in Dublin. He was educated at University College Cork, reading medieval history and archaeology. He later studied law and economics in University College Dublin. A year after winning the Patrick Kavanagh Award he published his first collection, *O Westport in the Light of Asia Minor*. Subsequent collections include *The Selected Paul Durcan*, *Cries of an Irish*

Caveman, and *The Berlin Wall Café*. He was commissioned to write verse impressions of several paintings in the National Gallery. His other works include *Greetings to Our friends in Brazil* and *The Laughter of Mothers*. He was awarded the Irish American Cultural Institute Poetry Award in 1989 and his collection *Daddy, Daddy* (1990) won the Whitbread Poetry Award. He was joint winner of the 1995 Heinemann Award. He is a member of Aosdána and lives in Dublin.

DUBLIN RECONSTRUCTED

There are several Dubliners who have written themselves into the history of the city through novels, autobiographies, plays and stories that give very real glimpses into the sociology and zeitgeist of the capital during the times in which they lived or live. Among these is

Paddy Crosbie
d.1982

who began writing sketches for various acts at the now defunct Theatre Royal. He was educated in North Brunswick Street Christian Brothers School. Later he returned as a teacher, eventually becoming the Principal. For years he hosted a hugely popular family radio show called 'The School Around the Corner.' His autobiographical *Your Dinner's Poured Out* was reviewed by the *Irish Press* with the accolade that he rebuilt a Dublin 'not only in bricks and stones, but in people, shops, churches, customs, ways and traditions that have long gone.' So too in their own way have the following.

Éamonn Mac Thomáis
1927-2002

was an IRA activist and editor of *An Phoblacht*, the nationalist newspaper. He lived in Golden Bridge, Inchicore. He left school at thirteen to work as a delivery boy for the White Heather Laundry on the South Circular Road and through this got to know Dublin's districts really well. He was imprisoned for IRA membership in August 1973, and was supported by protests from several writers including Peadar O'Donnell, Ulick O'Connor, Criostóir Ó Floinn and Dónall Mac Amhlaigh. He captured the feel, flavour and people of his city in his books, which include *Me Jewel and Darlin'*

Dublin, *Gur Cake & Coal Blocks*, both written while he was in prison, *Janey Mack Me Shirt is Black* and *Down Dublin Streets* (1916). He went on to run regular guided tours of his beloved city, enchanting tourists and natives alike with his witty anecdotes and yarns. He is buried in Glasnevin Cemetery.

Dublin had a thriving Jewish population in the early 1900s and much has been written about its customs and experiences. *Dublin's Little Jerusalem* by **Nick Harris d.2008** is a real celebration of the once-thriving and vibrant culture that centred around South Circular Road and Clanbrassil Street.

The first Jewish Mayor of Dublin, Ranelagh-born **Robert Emmet Briscoe** 1894-1969 wrote his autobiography *For the Life of Me* with Alden Hatch.

More recently **Asher Benson's** (1921-2006) *Jewish Dublin – Portraits of Life by the Liffey*, catalogued the characters and often their landmark business premises dotted around the city. He was an indefatigable activist and primary instigator of Dublin having its own Jewish Museum at 3 Walworth Road, off South Circular Road. A visit there will help followers of that most famous, albeit fictional Jew, Leopold Bloom, obtain a true insight into the cultural, economic, religious and social life of Dublin Jews during the 1900s. Leopold Bloom, the central character of James Joyce's *Ulysses* has been honoured by a plaque on 'his' house at 52 Clanbrassil Street, D8.

Elaine Crowley 1927-2011 wrote two memoirs – *Cowslips and Chainies* and *A Dublin Girl: Growing up in the 1930s* and numerous novels. Through these she shared a poignant and often funny capsule of tenement life in 1930s and early 1940s Dublin, showing how tightly knit communities in overcrowded living spaces worked, laughed and cried together, and for each other. She evoked the street games they used to play and the customs around First Communion days and the more sombre rituals of funerals and periods of mourning. She moved to Port Talbot in Wales many years ago.

Politician **C S 'Todd' Andrews** 1902-85 left his mark with his two volumes of autobiography *Dublin Made Me* and *A Man of No Property*. His descriptions bring alive the pre-independence Dublin in which he grew up and his progression into politics. He lived in Summerhill until 1910, when the family moved across town to the refined suburb of Terenure, which was considered to be in the country. Such experiences provided him with insights into two very different worlds. He recalls starting school with the nuns at St Saviour's Convent, Dominick Street, spending a very unhappy year at the school set up by Patrick Pearse, St Enda's in Rathfarnham, before going to the CBS in Synge Street. His accounts and observations of the times of the Rising and the War of Independence give clarity to the thinking behind divisions in families and factions. He is buried in Deansgrange Cemetery.

Entrepreneur **Bill Cullen 1942-** began his days in the slums of Summerhill in the 1940s, watching his Moore Street trader mother and equally feisty grandmother look after fourteen children while taking on the world. He sold apples and newspapers, Christmas decorations and flowers, anything to make money. In his bestelling book *It's a Long Way from Penny Apples* he vividly recaptures the poverty and deprivation, the struggles and challenges of slum life, as far removed from his later multi-millionaire success as could be imagined.

Comedian, scriptwriter and novelist **Brendan O'Carroll 1955-** was born in the north inner city, the youngest of eleven children. His mother, Maureen, was a Labour TD. He left school at twelve and had a string of occupations including waiter, milkman and DJ, before making the move to stand-up comedy. Much of his routines are about his childhood in Dublin city and in Finglas. He claims that his learning at the academy of life provided the material for six novels, many of which have sold internationally, and his comedy routines.

His 'Mrs Brown' character, who features centrally in his work, encapsulates much of the real life dramas and banalities he witnessed. Many of these were artfully portrayed in the film *Agnes Brown* - based on his book *The Mammy* - starring Anjelica Huston, who also directed. He has also written several stage plays and now a successful TV series, *Mrs Brown's Boys*. His other novels include *The Chisellers*, *The Granny*, *The Young Wan*, *Sparrow's Trap (The Scrapper)*.

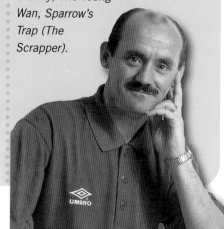

Anne Enright
1962-

Anne Enright is one of those writers who seem to know the profession from every angle. A pupil of St Louis High School in Rathmines and Trinity College, she has acted, written and produced plays for RTÉ, as well as short stories and novels. She blames it all on her parents, who gave her an electric typewriter for her twenty-first birthday. Those early tentative writings have blossomed and in 2007 she won the coveted Man Booker Prize for her book, *The Gathering*.

> MY DUBLIN – Anne Enright
> In other towns, clever people go out and make money. In Dublin, clever people go home and write their books.

Joseph Sheridan le Fanu
1814-73

Joseph Sheridan le Fanu came from Huguenot stock. He was born at 45 Dominick Street but moved when his father became chaplain at the Royal Hibernian Military School in the Phoenix Park (now St Mary's Hospital), settings which feature in some of his ghost stories. When he was twelve the family moved to Limerick, but Joseph returned to Dublin to attend Trinity College. In December 1844 he married Susanna Bennett, the daughter of a leading Dublin barrister. They took a house in Warrington Place near the Grand Canal. He eventually inherited a fine Georgian home, 15 Merrion Square. His wife died at the early age of thirty-four, leaving him with four young children. By this stage he had bought several publications, including *The Dublin University Magazine*, which had published his first short story, *The Ghost and the Bonesetter*. He set his first novel, *The House by the Graveyard*, in Chapelizod, close to where he had grown up. He completed numerous other novels, including *Mr Justice Harbottle*, also known as *An Account of Some Strange Disturbances in Aungier Street*. *Carmilla* caused a stir for its lesbian vampire theme and it has also served as the inspiration for several movies, including Hammer's *The Vampire Lovers* (1970) and Roger Vadim's *Blood and Roses*. His collection of short stories *In a Glass Darkly*, was published the year before he died. Both his grandmother, Alicia Sheridan Le Fanu, and his great-uncle, Richard Brinsley Sheridan, were playwrights. He is buried in Mount Jerome Cemetery.

Peter Fallon
1951-

A Trinity College Dublin alumnus, Peter Fallon went on to have a big impact on publishing in Ireland. An Honours Graduate, in 1994 he was Writer Fellow in the English Department. At the age of eighteen he founded the Gallery Press in Oldcastle County Meath. This has published hundreds of books of poetry and plays by some of the country's finest authors including Derek Mahon, John Montague, Nuala Ní Dhomhnaill, Ciaran Carson, Medbh McGuckian, John Banville, Eiléan Ní Chuilleanáin and Paul Muldoon.

Peter Fallon's own collections include *The Speaking Stones, Winter Work, The News and Weather, Eye To Eye* and *The Company of Horses.*

Bernard Farrell
1939-

Playwright Bernard Farrell grew up in Sandycove and attended the Christian Brothers School in Monkstown. After the success of *I do Not Like Thee Doctor Fell* in the Abbey Theatre in 1979, Farrell decided to give up the day job and write fulltime. Since then he has written twenty-two plays, most of which have premiered at either the Gate or the Abbey theatres. His hits include *Stella by Starlight, Canaries, Say Cheese, The Last Apache Reunion* and *Bookworms. The Verdi Girls* was commissioned by the Laguna Playhouse in California. Farrell has won numerous awards for his work including the Rooney Prize for Irish Literature and the Sunday Tribune Comedy Prize of the Year.

Sir Samuel Ferguson
1810-86

Belfast poet and barrister and Trinity graduate, Samuel Ferguson made his home in Dublin. Ill-health after he was called to the Bar sent him on the Grand Tour of Europe, making him even more interesting company on his return. He became know for his erudite delivery, his gregarious nature and for his marvellous salons that always guaranteed the best of gracious hospitality and intelligent discourse. Ferguson lived in 11 Henrietta Street until he married Mary Catherine, a grandniece of Arthur Guinness. After their wedding in St Brigid's Church in Stillorgan they resided in Howth, County Dublin, then at 9 Gloucester Street (now Sean Mac Dermott Street), before moving to 20 North Great George's Street, a place their friends jokingly referred to as the 'Ferguson Arms' because it was such an open house.

Literary evenings and soirees were commonplace. Ferguson even wrote condensed versions of some of Shakespeare's plays for the delectation of his guests. These were published in a volume as *Shakespearean Breviates*.

He stopped practising law when he was appointed first Deputy Keeper of the Public Records, a post that led to a knighthood in 1878. Four years later he was elected first President of the Royal Irish Academy. In a paper he delivered to that body he proposed that it would be possible and preferable to construct a tunnel under the River Liffey to accommodate the railway line, rather than obstruct the view along the river to Gandon's splendid Custom's House with an overhead loop line. His suggestion was ignored then, but how right he was!

The Fergusons returned to Howth when Samuel's health began to fail and rented Strand Lodge on Claremont Road, where he died. As a token of the esteem in which he was held, his funeral service took place in St Patrick's Cathedral and a plaque was later erected there to commemorate him. He is buried in the churchyard of St John's, Donegore, County Antrim. Among his poetry is *Aideen's Grave*, *The Cromlech of Howth* and *The Quest*

of Dermid. He also wrote the songs *The Lark in the Clear Air* and *The Coolin*.

George Fitzmaurice
1877-1963

Fitzmaurice worked in the Land Commission in Dublin. He wrote *The Country Dressmaker*, *The Pie-dish* and *Country Glasses*, but fell out with Yeats and Lady Gregory when they stopped accepting his plays at the Abbey Theatre. However he had the last word by having 'late Abbey Playwright' inscribed on his tombstone in Mount Jerome Cemetery.

In Appreciation We Remember
GEORGE FITZMAURICE
LATE ABBEY PLAYWRIGHT
OF DUAGH AND DUBLIN.
1877 – 1963

ERECTED BY
DUAGH HISTORICAL SOCIETY
IN ASSOCIATION WITH
NORTH KERRY LITERARY TRUST

Gerard Mannix Flynn
1957-

Gerard Mannix Flynn, actor and author, was born in Dublin and at the age of eleven was sent to St Joseph's Industrial School in Letterfrack, Co Donegal. There Flynn suffered physical and sexual abuse and later spent time in the Central Mental Hospital in Dundrum. He was also a detainee in both Marlborough House Detention Centre and St Patrick's

Institution, Mountjoy. These experiences are reflected in his works. *The Liberty Suite*, co-written with Peter Sheridan, premiered at the Dublin Theatre Festival with Flynn himself playing the part of the hero. *Talking to the Wall* was commissioned by the Abbey Theatre in 1990 and was also performed by the author at the Edinburgh Festival where it won a Scotsman's Fringe First Award in 1997.

He told his story in *Nothing to Say* and in his semi-autobiographical play, *James X*. By this time the abuse in state institutions was well documented – his protagonist sues the government as he comes to terms with what had been inflicted on him. Flynn appeared in the films *When the Sky Falls* and *Cal*. He is a member of Aosdána and was elected to Dublin City Council in 2009.

Carlo Gébler
1954-

Dublin-born Carlo Gébler is the son of writers Ernest Gébler and Edna O'Brien (*see p157*). He has written numerous novels, travel books and stories for children. His novels include *The Eleventh Summer*, *August in July* and *How To Murder a Man*. In 2000 he published an autobiography entitled *Father and I*. He now lives outside Enniskillen in Northern Ireland and teaches

creative writing at HMP Maghaberry, where he is writer-in-residence. He is a member of Aosdána and was on the board of the Arts Council from 1999 to 2003.

Ernest Gébler
1915-98

The son of an Austro-Hungarian musician who had settled in Ireland and a Dublin mother who worked as a cinema usherette, Ernest Gébler was born here and wrote several books and plays. *The Plymouth Adventure: The Voyage of the Mayflower* was his most successful. It sold five million copies and was filmed by MGM, starring Lloyd Bridges and Spencer Tracy. Another of his books, *Hoffman*, also known as *Shall I Eat You Now?* was also turned into a movie, starring Sinéad Cusack and Peter Sellers. Gébler was married to writer Edna O'Brien (*see p157*) and was a member of Aosdána.

Monk Gibbon
1896-1987

Poet, novelist and brilliant raconteur, Monk Gibbon was born in the now demolished glebe house at St Naithi's Church, Dundrum when his father was canon there. He attended St Columba's College (later William Trevor's alma mater). He went to Oxford, but after only one term he volunteered for the army and while on leave in Ireland he witnessed an event at Portobello Barracks which led to him writing the memoir *Inglorious Soldier*. This gives a first-hand account of the shooting of the pacifist Francis Sheehy Skeffington during the 1916 Rising. (Skeffington's close friends at UCD were James Joyce and Thomas Kettle).

In 1926 Gibbon had his first volume of poetry published. This was called *The Tremulous String*, followed a year later by *The Branch of the Hawthorn Tree*. After travelling and teaching in Ireland, Wales and Switzerland he settled with his wife Winifred and six children in Tara Hall, Sandycove Road, Dun Laoghaire. Their afternoon tea parties, often with poetry readings, were attended by a goodly mix of the Dublin literati whom Monk Gibbon counted among his friends.

He hadn't got the same relationship with his cousin, William Butler Yeats, whom he portrayed in a rather hostile fashion in his biography *The Masterpiece and the Man: Yeats as I Knew Him*. In response, Yeats commented, 'Monk Gibbon is one of the three people in Dublin whom I dislike ... because he is argumentative!'

After forty years in Sandycove the Gibbons moved to Killiney, but he remained a familiar figure in Sandycove, cycling everywhere well into his eighties. He is buried in the cemetery beside St Naithi's. The inscription reads 'Sing In That Scented Night, Invisibly, And as you always do/Sing sweetly.' (Yeats's sisters, Lolly and Lily, are also buried in this little graveyard).

Sir John Gilbert
1829-98

was the librarian at the Royal Irish Academy for thirty years. During that time he wrote *History of the City of Dublin* and *History of the Viceroys of Ireland*. He bequeathed his extensive personal library to Pearse Street Library and Archive.

Oliver St John Gogarty
1878-1957

Poet, raconteur and wit, Oliver St John Gogarty was born at 5 Rutland Square East, but the family later moved to Fairfield in Glasnevin. He went to the CBS at North Richmond Street, where Tom Kettle was also a pupil, and then to Clongowes Wood School in County Kildare. He used to cycle to Dublin and back to play football for Bohemians. He studied medicine in the Catholic

University Medical School in Cecelia Street and at Trinity College, before taking time off to attend Worcester College Oxford, in pursuit of the Newdigate Poetry Prize, which Oscar Wilde had won six years previously. Unsuccessful, he returned to his medical studies. Shortly before that he had met James Joyce in the National Library, Kildare Street. While at Oxford Gogarty met Dermot Trench, who many believe was the prototype for Haines in *Ulysses*, and the trio moved in together in the Martello Tower in Sandycove, Co Dublin, across from the famous Forty Foot, then a 'men only' bathing place, where Gogarty often swam three or four times a day. Joyce's stay was short-lived, although he

did immortalise the tower as the opening setting for *Ulysses*.

Gogarty became an ear, nose and throat specialist. He bought a stylish home and consulting rooms at 15 Ely Place, (now the Royal Hibernian Academy) and an equally stylish yellow Rolls Royce. George Moore and Bram Stoker's brother, surgeon Sir Thornly Stoker, were his neighbours.

In 1917 Gogarty had his first play *Blight* produced at the Abbey Theatre, followed closely by *A Serious Thing* and *The Enchanted Trousers*.

Gogarty was an IRA supporter and allowed his home to be used as a safe house. He was kidnapped and taken to a hideaway

Top: The Oliver St John Gogarty pub in Temple Bar.
Above: Key to the Martello Tower in Sandycove

beside the River Liffey at Chapelizod. He escaped into the garden, dived into the water and was carried to safety by the freezing flow. Sometime later he ceremonially released two swans into the river, witnessed by his wife, WB Yeats and W T Cosgrave, President of the Executive Council of the Irish Free State. He also wrote a collection of poems, *An Offering of Swans*.

Writers who regularly gathered on Friday nights at the Gogarty house included James Stephens, Yeats, Tom Kettle, George Moore, Lord Dunsany, Lennox Robinson, Seumas O'Sullivan and AE. He revealed some of what went on in Ely Place in *As I Was Going Down Sackville Street*, which led to a libel case against him, in which Samuel Beckett was a witness for the prosecution. He also published *I Follow St. Patrick*, *Tumbling in the Hay* and *Elbow Room*, a collection of poetry.

He, in turn, initiated a libel suit against Patrick Kavanagh who had written in his autobiography '*I mistook Gogarty's white-robed maid for his wife or his mistress*'.

Gogarty was awarded £100 in damages.

When war broke out he tried to enlist as a doctor with the RAF and RAMC, but at fifty-one he was turned down, so he went to the US, leaving his family in their Galway home at Renvyle. There his writings included *Rolling Down the Lea* and *It Isn't this Time of Year At All!* He died in the US but was brought back to Galway to be buried.

Oliver Goldsmith
1728-74

Although Oliver Goldsmith spent only five years in Dublin, he is a highly visible resident of the capital by virtue of having one of the only two statues in the front grounds of Trinity College (*see photo*). He was certainly not an A-student. He started out studying law and theology and came bottom of his year. It took him five years to graduate as a Bachelor of Arts. He travelled extensively in Europe, busking with a flute to stay solvent, before he turned to journalism. His most famous novel is *The Vicar of Wakefield*; his best-known poem *The Deserted Village* and his best play *She*

GOLDSMITH

Stoops to Conquer which was produced at Covent Garden in 1773. He died the following year and is buried in the churchyard at The Temple, off Fleet Street, in London. His epitaph, which was written by Samuel Johnson, includes the famous line: *Nullum quod tetigit non ornavit - He touched nothing that he did not adorn.*

Lady Gregory
1852-1932

Isabella Augusta Persse was the twelfth child of sixteen, born into a privileged class and a stately home in County Galway. All through her life she was to try and better the lives of those less fortunate. She married at twenty-seven. Her husband, Sir William Gregory, was thirty-six years her senior. She took several lovers during her life, but when her husband died she went into black for the rest of her days. She and WB Yeats met and he became a regular visitor for twenty summers to her home at Coole Park. The house where she entertained notable writers of the time is no more, having been demolished in 1941. In its heyday Lady Gregory's guests included Sean O'Casey, John Millington Synge, Padraic Colum and George Bernard Shaw. The estate, with its 'seven woods' is still very much intact, and so too is the famous 'autograph tree' where many of the aforementioned carved their initials on an old beech.

No doubt their conversations and interest in a revival of Celtic art, language and literature were the cause of much passionate debate and resolve, leading in part to the founding of the Irish National

The Abbey Theatre

Theatre, the Abbey, in 1904. Lady Gregory became not only a sponsor, benefactor, and board member but also the author of forty plays, translator and collector of poems, ballads, sagas and folktales, many of which she translated from Irish. She was instrumental in taking the Abbey Theatre Company to America in 1911-12 and remained very involved until her death in 1932. She is buried beside her sister, Annabelle, in Bohermore Cemetery in Galway.

While in Dublin she stayed at the Gresham Hotel in O'Connell Street. Her works include *Gods and Fighting Men*, *Visions and Beliefs in the West of Ireland*, *Spreading the News*, *The Workhouse Ward* and *The Rising of the Moon*.

Her only son, Robert, born a year after her marriage to Sir William Gregory, is the airman referred to in W B Yeats's poem *An Irish Airman Foresees his Death*. Robert, a major in the Royal Flying Corps, was killed in 1918 when shot down over Italy.

Hugo Hamilton
1953-

Hugo Hamilton was born in Dublin of a German mother and Irish father. At home the only languages that were spoken were Irish and German so he looked on English as a bit of a challenge. He became a journalist and went on to write numerous novels and a memoir, *The Speckled People*, which was shortlisted for an Irish Book of the Decade 2000-2010. His novels include *Sucking Diesel* and *Hand in the Fire*, as well as two detective novels set in Dublin, *Headbanger* and *The Sad Bastard*. He won the Rooney Prize for Irish Literature in 1992.

Michael Hartnett
1941-99

A native of Limerick, Michael Hartnett attended UCD briefly and then headed to England. His first book, *Anatomy of a Cliché*, got him noticed in a wider circle. At various stages he worked as a tea boy on a building site, in the telephone exchange as a night telephonist and also as a curator at the Joyce Tower in Sandycove, Co Dublin. Moving back to Limerick in 1974 he penned *A Farewell to English*, detailing his intention to write only in Irish in the future. This he did for a while, producing such collections as *Adharca Broic*, *An Phurgóid* and *Do Nuala: Foighne Chrainn*. Unfortunately, alcoholism took hold of his life and eventually caused his premature death. After the breakup of his marriage he returned to Dublin in 1968. He published his volume *Inchicore Haiku* while living in that neighbourhood. He continued to work in the two languages and left a fine body of translations into English, including *Bruadair, Selected Poems of Daibhi Ó Bruadair and Ó Rathaille – The Poems of Aodhaghán Ó Rathaille*. He followed these with *Collected Poems* and *New and Selected Poems*. He died in 1999 and is buried at Calvary Cemetery, Newcastle West, County Limerick. A new *Collected Poems* appeared posthumously in 2001.

Anne Haverty
1959-

Journalist, novelist and biographer Anne Haverty was born in Tipperary, but lives in Dublin. Her first novel, *One Day as a Tiger*, won the Rooney Prize for Irish Literature in 1997. Her other novels include *The Far Side of a Kiss* and *The Free and Easy*. Her poetry is collected as *The Beauty of the Moon*. She has also written a biography of Constance Markievicz and is one of the writers featured in *Ladies Night at Finbarr's Hotel*. She is a member of Aosdána.

Seamus Heaney
1939-

The internationally-renowned poet, writer and lecturer was born in Northern Ireland but lives in Dublin, where he spent several years teaching at Carysfort College before becoming its Head of English. That was followed by periods as writer in residence and taking professorships at various universities around the world, including Harvard and Oxford. He has had numerous accolades showered upon him for his vast body of work, but the most prestigious has to be the Nobel Prize in Literature, which he was awarded in 1995. He also won two Whitbread prizes, in 1996 and 1999, and was made Commandeur de l'Ordre des Arts et Lettres in 1996. His poetry collections include *The Spirit Level*, *Electric Light*, *The Human Chain* and *District and Circle*, which got him the T S Elliott Prize. Heaney also wrote plays, numerous translations and prose.

MY DUBLIN – Seamus Heaney

At first, Dublin was the adventure of journeys from County Derry to Croke Park for GAA finals and semi-finals, then of trips as a student to the Gate Theatre and the Abbey, then literary pubs and poets in the 1960s and 1970s and now the constant view of Sandymount Strand and the image of Stephen Dedalus out there striding into eternity.

Excerpt from Viking Dublin: Trial Pieces by Seamus Heaney (from *North* and *Opened Ground*, Faber & Faber)

II

These are trial pieces,
the craft's mystery
improvised on bone:
foliage, bestiaries,

interlacings elaborate
as the netted routes
of ancestry and trade.
That have to be

magnified on display
so that the nostril
is a migrant prow
sniffing the Liffey,

swanning it up to the ford,
dissembling itself
in antler combs, bone pins,
coins, weights, scale-pans.

III

Like a long sword
sheathed in its moisting
burial clays,
the keel stuck fast

in the slip of the bank,
its clinker-built hull
spined and plosive
as *Dublin*.

And now we reach in
for shards of the vertebrae,
the ribs of hurdle,
the mother-wet caches –

and for this trial piece
incised by a child,
a longship, a buoyant
migrant line.

IV

That enters my longhand,
turns cursive, unscarfing
a zoomorphic wake,
a worm of thought

I follow into the mud.
I am Hamlet the Dane,
skull-handler, parablist,
smeller of rot

in the state, infused
with its poisons,
pinioned by ghosts
and affections,

murders and pieties,
coming to consciousness
by jumping in graves,
dithering, blathering.

VI

'Did you ever hear tell,'
says Jimmy Farrell,
'of the skulls they have
in the city of Dublin?

White skulls and black skulls
and yellow skulls, and some
with full teeth, and some
haven't only but one,'

and compounded history
in the pan of 'an old Dane,
maybe, was drowned
in the Flood.'

My words lick around
cobbled quays, go hunting
lightly as pampooties
over the skull-capped ground.

Lafcadio Hearn
1850-1904

Born on the Greek island of Lefkas,
of a Greek mother and an Irish
father. Patrick Lafcadio Hearn grew
up in Dublin, first at 48 Lower
Gardiner Street and then at 21
Leinster Square, Rathmines. He also
lived at 3 Prince Terrace, Rathmines
and 73 Upper Leeson Street. Very
self-conscious of his appearance
after losing an eye in an accident
while in St Cuthbert's College in
Ushaw, Durham, he always posed in
profile for photographs. On moving
to Japan he totally embraced its
culture, its writings and its way of
life and went on to become regarded
as a very important writer. He is
remembered with a monument at
Matsue, where he lived for a time,
and in Ireland at the Sundai Ireland
International School in County
Kildare. His work is on the
curriculum of schools in Japan.
Much of it focuses on legends and
ghost stories such as *Kwaidan:
Stories and Studies of Strange
Things*. He didn't forget his Irish
roots however, and in his story, *The
Dream of a Summer Day* the
influences of one of Yeats's early
poems *The Wanderings of Oisín* are
evident.

In Ian Fleming's 1964 *You Only
Live Twice* James Bond replies to
his arch enemy Blofeld's comment,
'Have you ever heard the Japanese
expression *kirisute gomen?*'
('authorisation to cut and leave'.
Samurai had the right to strike at

anyone of a lower class who was compromising their honour) with 'Spare me the Lafcadio Hearn, Blofeld.'

Hearn was cremated and his ashes are buried in Zoshigaya Cemetery in Toyko.

Felicia Hemans
1793-1835

Calm on the bosom of thy God,
Fair spirit rest thee now!
E'en while with us thy footsteps trod,
His seal was on thy brow.
Dust, to its narrow house beneath!
Soul, to its place on high,
They may have seen thy look in death
No more may fear to die

These words of poet Felicia Dorothea (Browne) Hemans are inscribed where she is buried in the crypt of St Anne's Church in Dawson Street, where she was a parishioner. There's also a stained glass window in the church dedicated to her memory. She came to Dublin from Liverpool when she married her Irish husband, Captain Hemans of the King's Own Regiment. Later and without her husband, although it's not known if she had been widowed or just separated, and a mother of five sons by twenty-five,

she moved back to Dublin where a younger brother lived. She resided on Upper Pembroke Street, then at 36 St Stephen's Green. She wrote profusely and was popular in the United States too. She counted Sir Walter Scott and William Wordsworth among her friends and had stayed with the latter in his home in the Lake District the year before she left England. When she died, at 21 Dawson Street, Wordsworth and Walter Savage Landor wrote verses in her honour.

Her best remembered work is possibly *Casabianca*, which opens with the memorable lines:

The boy stood on the burning deck
Whence all but he had fled;
The flame that lit the battle's wreck
Shone round him o'er the dead.

F R Higgins
1896-1941

Born in Mayo, Frederick 'Fred' R Higgins grew up in Meath, left school at fourteen, and home at sixteen, after a disagreement with his father about their politics. He went into lodgings at 20 North Clarence Street, North Strand, Dublin. He got a job in Brooks Thomas Builders' Providers, where he met his future wife, the harpist

Beatrice May. He met Austin Clarke at this time and became a protégée of WB Yeats. Through them he gained acceptance into literary circles and met George Moore, AE and Padraic Ó Conaire. His poetry was beginning to get noticed and he was published. He went on to become a founding member and secretary of the Irish Academy of Letters. Having spent three years in Mayo, he and Beatrice returned to Dublin in 1932, where they moved to Doddervale in Rathfarnham. He became a director of the Abbey Theatre in 1935 and his *Deuce of Jacks*, a one-act comedy, was staged there. Two years later he took the Abbey Company to the US and Canada and was subsequently appointed its managing director. He published several books of poetry including *Island Blood*, *The Dark Breed*, *Arable Holdings* and *The Gap of Brightness*.

He is buried in a family plot in the privately owned graveyard at Laracor church in County Meath.

Gerard Manley Hopkins
1844-89

Gerard Manley Hopkins was an English poet who converted to Roman Catholicism and became a Jesuit priest. He spent the last five years of his life in Dublin where he taught Greek and Latin in the Catholic University at 86 St Stephen's Green. Melancholy a lot of the time, he suffered frequent bouts of depression. He contracted typhoid fever in 1989 and died. A conflicted man, he sometimes burnt his work and at one stage resolved never to have his poetry published. Indeed, he published very little during his lifetime and it was only posthumously that he achieved fame. He never quite came to terms with the Irish or with Dublin, which he described as 'a joyless place'. Ironically, his last words are reported to have been, 'I am so happy, I am so happy. I loved my life.' His funeral Mass was celebrated in the Church of Saint Francis Xavier in Gardiner Street, followed by a burial in the Jesuit plot in Glasnevin Cemetery.

Paul Howard
1971-

Journalist Paul Howard grew up in Ballybrack, Co Dublin. He was a journalist and then chief sports writer for the *Sunday Tribune*, winning Sports Journalist of the Year in the 1998 Irish Media

Awards. He is now best known for his fictional creation, *Ross O'Carroll-Kelly*, the Dublin 4 rugby jock, snob and wannabe. (The D4 postal district houses many of the wealthy who share, according to Ross, an insatiable desire to have the biggest, the most and the best of everything). His satirical and bored look at life, written in the first person, became an instant success when he appeared as a column in the *Sunday Tribune,* later transferring to *The Irish Times.* To date he has spawned over ten bestselling books, the first being *The Miseducation of Ross O'Carroll-Kelly*, two plays, *The Last Days of the Celtic Tiger* and *Between Blackrock and a Hard Place*, with more to come. The *Oh My God Delusion*, the tenth novel in the Ross series, won the Best Popular Fiction Award in the 2010 Bord Gais Irish Book Awards.

Howard has also written several non-fiction books, including *The Joy, Celtic Warrior* and *The Gaffers.*

Douglas Hyde
1860-1949

Roscommon-born Douglas Hyde (Dubhglas de hÍde) was a noted champion of the Irish language, a folklorist, a playwright, a poet and a founder member of the Gaelic League, established in 1893 with the aim of restoring the Irish language and of de-Anglicising Ireland. He studied at Trinity College, where he had rooms at number 24 on the ground floor. He took a full and active role, becoming involved with the Theological and Historical Societies as well as the chess club. His play *Casadh an tSúgáin* was the first play ever to be staged in Irish, opening at the Gaiety Theatre in South King Street in 1901. Lady Gregory later translated it into English. Hyde became the first Professor of Modern Irish at UCD in 1909. His diaries reveal friendships and meetings with Yeats, Katherine Tynan, George Sigerson, John O'Leary and Maud Gonne. In 1890 he published his first collection of Irish folktales, entitled *Beside the Fire*, and used a pseudonym for other poetry, writing as *An Craoibhín Aoibhinn*, (The Delightful Little Branch). Hyde also founded the National Literary Society in Dublin.

Hyde became Ireland's first President in 1938 and although he suffered ill health from early on in his seven-year term he continued in office until 1945. During this period he lived in the former Viceregal Lodge in the Phoenix Park, now called *Áras an Uachtaráin (Presidential Residence)*. There's a bronze bust of Hyde in the contemporary art gallery in Trinity College, which is called the Douglas Hyde Gallery. He also has also a memorial in Christ Church Cathedral.

Maeve Ingoldsby
1947-

Maeve Ingoldsby, who lives in Portmarnock, County Dublin, is a playwright and scriptwriter. She has written a long list of plays for young people, two children's operas, numerous pantomimes and satirical revues and scripts for radio and TV. A former writer for the RTÉ radio show *Only Slaggin'* she was also a writer on its long-running television soaps, *Glenroe* and *Fair City*. Her children's play *Earwigs* was awarded 'Best Young People's Production' at the Dublin Theatre Festival in 1995.

Pat Ingoldsby
1942-

Describing himself as a 'chronicler of life', Pat Ingoldsby's often quirky poetry in both Irish and English has been widely influenced by his native city. Although well known previously for his television work he is now more likely to be found selling his books of poetry and maybe even reciting a few lines too on the streets of Dublin. You'll find him easily as he uses handwritten signs to advertise – with messages like – *Live Irish Writer – not dead yet. Sorry!* and *Health Warning ALL my poems contain IMAGINATION!* His collections include *Do Lámh I Mo Bhrístí*, *Can I Get In The Bath?* and *I Thought You Died Years Ago*. He lives in Clontarf.

John Kells Ingram
1823-1907

Born in Donegal, John Kells Ingram was having sonnets published in the *Dublin University Magazine* when he was just sixteen. He matriculated at Trinity College at age fourteen, an entrée that would see him spending the next fifty-five years of his esteemed academic and very distinguished career at that university. He was never far away, as he lived in 38 Upper Mount Street. His interests were varied: he was President of the Library Association of Great Britain, co-founder of the National Library of Ireland, Vice-president of the Library Association of Ireland and a member of the Royal Irish Academy, among other things. He was very interested in fostering education for young ladies and played a seminal role in the setting up of Alexandra College which opened at number 6 Earlsfort Terrace. It moved to its current complex in Dublin 6 in 1972.

On the literary front he is reputed to have 'quickly dashed off a political ballad' entitled *The Memory of the Dead*. That poem is well remembered for its opening:-

Who fears to speak of Ninety-eight?
Who blushes at the name?
When cowards mock the patriot's fate,
Who hangs his head for shame?

Although the complete poem was published anonymously in Thomas Davis's *The Nation* newspaper, it was an open secret who had penned it.

Ingram was selected to write entries for two of the most famous editions of the *Encyclopaedia Britannica*. He wrote 'the scholars' entries that appeared in the ninth and the eleventh editions.

He also wrote the novel, *Amelia's Escape from theTomb* or *Escape from the Tomb (see illustration)*. He is buried in Mount Jerome Cemetery, Harold's Cross.

AMELIA'S ESCAPE FROM THE TOMB.
page 18.

Thomas Caulfield Irwin
1823-92

Originally from County Down, poet and novelist Thomas Caulfield Irwin found work on *The Irish People*, John O'Leary's Fenian newspaper, in 12 Parliament Street, Dublin. He wrote abundantly, submitting copy to *The Bell*, the *Dublin Magazine* and to *The Nation*.

Irwin loved his cats and when one went missing he advertised: 'Robbery! One pound reward. Stolen from the back drawing room at 1 Portland Street, North Circular Road, Dublin, between the hours of one and three o'clock on Saturday 5th June 1872, a large Dark Grey and Black Male Cat, the property of Mr Thomas C. Irwin. The poor animal, who answers to the name of Tom, and is lame in the left forepaw and weak in the left eye, can be of no value to anyone but Mr Irwin, who had him for five years before he lost him through the cruel and desperate act of a miscreant. One pound will be given by me to whoever restores the animal uninjured, and at once, to the above address, or who affords authentic information as to the party who entered Mr Irwin's room and committed the robbery.'

There is no record of whether he got Tom back, but almost a decade later another notice appeared, this time seeking the return of 'Two grey brindled striped cats' which had gone missing, this time from his 41 St Stephen's Green address.

The cats weren't the only ones who were unhappy with Mr Irwin. His next-door neighbour, John O'Donovan wrote to Samuel Ferguson, poet and antiquarian: 'I understand that the mad poet, (Irwin) claims acquaintance with you. He says I am his enemy, and watch him through the thickness of the wall that divides our houses. He threatens in consequence to shoot me. One of us must leave. I have a house full of books and children; he has an umbrella and a revolver. If, under the circumstances, you could use your influence and persuade him to remove to other quarters, you would confer a great favour on, yours faithfully, John O'Donovan.'

It's not clear if that worked, but when Irwin died, ten years later, he was living at 36 Upper Mount Pleasant Avenue, Rathmines. He is buried in Mount Jerome Cemetery.

His works include prose and eight volumes of verse as well as a biography of Swift.

Denis Johnston
1901-84

Denis Johnston of Wellington Road and Lansdowne Road, Dublin 4, was one of the many playwrights whose work was rejected by Lady Gregory for staging at the Abbey. She turned down his *Shadowdance* so he changed its name, took it to the Gate and it was produced by Hilton Edwards as *The Old Lady Says No!* Micheál MacLiammóir, who played the Speaker in it, reputedly said it was as satisfying as playing Hamlet. Johnston had obviously impressed the two founders of the Gate, because when he presented his second play, *The Moon in the Yellow River*, he was asked to become a director of the theatre, a position he

DENIS JOHNSTON 1901-1984 and his wife BETTY CHANCELLOR 1910-1984

Strumpet City in the sunset
Wilful city of savage dreamers,
So old, so sick with memories!
Old Mother
Some they say are damned,
But you, I know, will walk
the streets of Paradise
Head high, and unashamed

held until 1936. He relocated to England where he became a BBC war correspondent and later Director of Programmes for the BBC Television Service. He moved to the US, producing Yeats and Shaw at Smith when he was Head of Drama. His grudge against the Abbey seems to have been erased when, in 1958, it produced *The Scythe and the Sunset*, his play about the Easter Rising.

Johnston returned to Dublin where he lived in 8 Sorrento Terrace. He continued to write and lecture and was given an Honorary Doctorate from the New University of Ulster. His work includes a biographical study *In Search of Swift*. He is buried with his wife, Betty Chancellor, in St Patrick's Close, beside the Cathedral (*see photo opposite*). At his request the church bells were rung on the occasion of his funeral and his tombstone engraved with seven lines from the play that made his name – *The Old Lady Says No!* They read:

Strumpet city in the sunset
Wilful city of savage dreamers,
So old, so sick with memories
Old Mother;
Some they are damned,
But you, I know, will walk the
streets of Paradise
Head high, and unashamed.

Jennifer Johnston
1930-

Jennifer Johnson is the daughter of Denis Johnston. Born in Dublin and educated at Trinity College, she now lives in Derry and has written fifteen novels and five plays. *Her Shadows on Our Skin* was shortlisted for the Booker Prize in 1977 and in 1979 *The Old Jest* won her the Whitbread Award. *The Old Jest*, a novel about the Irish War of Independence, was subsequently made into a film starring Anthony Hopkins, entitled *The Dawning*.

Neil Jordan
1950-

Although the novelist and filmmaker was born in Sligo he was brought up in Dublin and educated at St Paul's College in Raheny, and later at UCD, where he studied Irish History and Literature. His movies include *The Miracle* and Patrick McCabe's *The Butcher Boy*. *The Crying Game*, which he wrote and directed, was nominated for six Academy Awards, winning the one for Best Original Screenplay. His novels include *Sunrise with Sea Monster*, *The Past*, *Shade*, *Mistaken* and a collection of short stories – *Night in Tunisia*.

James Joyce
1882 -1941

Arguably one of Ireland's best-known writers worldwide, Joyce was born at 41 Brighton Square, Rathgar, a very fashionable address. His parents later moved to 23 Castlewood Avenue in Rathmines. Three of Joyce's siblings were born here and were delivered by a Mrs Thornton who later appeared in *Ulysses*. (Leopold Bloom sends for her to deliver Milly, his daughter).

They then moved to a Martello Tower in County Wicklow where four more children were born. At the age of six and half James was sent as a boarder to Clongowes Wood College. He only stayed there for three years because his father lost his well-paid job and, in fact, was never to work again.

They moved to 23 Carysfort Avenue and stayed there for a year in a house called Leoville that is still extant. In his semi-autobiographical book *A Portrait of the Artist as a Young Man* he mentions the local church of St John and the nearby park. It was here too that he wrote *Et Tu Hanly*, his first recorded work. His proud father had it printed up for him. Their next home was in 19 Hardwicke Street, which is no more,

and again Joyce uses this in *The Boarding House* in *Dubliners*. Months later they were on the move again.

John Stanislaus Joyce's money went on drink rather than rent and as soon as the landlords caught up with him he moved his large family on. He got involved with moneylenders, one of whom appears as Reuben Dodd in *Ulysses*.

A fortuitous meeting between a Jesuit of his father's acquaintance led to an offer to educate the Joyce boys free at Belvedere College in Great Denmark Street. (This priest is the Father Conmee who appears in *The Wandering Rocks*). James did well at school, winning scholarships along the way. The Jesuits hoped that they had found a recruit for the priesthood but he opted to study medicine instead. Because of lack of money he had to withdraw from Catholic University Medical School and headed to Paris, hoping to continue his studies there. He returned shortly afterwards because his mother was dying.

In 1903 he met Nora Barnacle, a chambermaid from Galway. He also met Oliver St John Gogarty who invited him to stay in Sandycove in his Martello Tower, the setting for

The Martello Tower in Sandycove, now the Joyce Museum

the opening scenes in *Ulysses*. But, after 'an incident' with a gun in the first week Joyce was asked to leave so he and Nora departed to Europe, settling first in Trieste and later in Paris. During the wars they moved to Switzerland and lived in Zurich. They married in 1931 and had two children, Giorgio and Lucia. Although Joyce never returned to Ireland after 1912, he wrote about Dublin 'the centre of paralysis' constantly. He also included many places from his childhood, and listed many of his former addresses in *Finnegan's Wake*. He died in Zurich and is buried there in Fluntern Cemetery. Nora was buried nearby. In 1966 the lease on Joyce's grave expired but the authorities decided to honour the couple by reuniting them and they now lie together.

James Joyce's writings were not an instant success with publishers, often leading to protracted battles with the fraternity. Sylvia Beach published *Ulysses* in 1922 (*see title page, left*) and was taken to court in the US by John Sumner, the Secretary of the Prevention of Vice, as it was deemed to be obscene. Copies were intercepted by the US Postal Service and burned, and the publishers fined.

A series of fourteen Robin Buick brass pavement plaques denote places on the *Ulysses* trail from O'Connell Street to Kildare Street, Dublin, and there is a bust of the author in St Stephen's Green.

BLOOMSDAY

James Joyce wrote *Ulysses* for Nora Barnacle, chronicling the day they had their first date, 16 June 1904. The book is a parallel to Homer's *Odyssey*, written in eighteen episodes. Each chapter is told from a different viewpoint. In 1954, fifty years after the date on which it was set, poets Patrick Kavanagh and Anthony Cronin, along with a few other friends, decided to mark the event by making the journey to the Martello Tower in Sandycove to retrace the steps of Leopold Bloom on that day – thus the commemorative day now referred to as Bloomsday was born.

Since then it's become something of a pilgrimage for Joyce aficionados from home and abroad who don period costume and gather to join in re-enacting the walk, engage in lively debate, read or act out passages from the sequences, and of course socialize at some of the hostelries mentioned in the book. Some even enjoy the famous breakfast fare at the Bailey – *'the grilled mutton kidneys which gave to his (Leopold Blooms') palate a fine tang of faintly scented urine,'* or stop off for a Gorgonzola sandwich and a glass of Burgundy at Davy Byrne's.

Bloomsday has now stretched into a four-day festival, with readings, walks and other convivial activities that all connect in some way with *Ulysses,* so no matter where you are in Dublin city or county there is bound to be some Joyce-related activity in which you can get involved.

Bloomsday walks are organised through Dublin Tourism www.visitdublin.com or you can download a free podcast audio iWalk **'In the Steps of Ulysses'** at www.visitdublin.com/iwalks. The James Joyce Centre (*see page 206*) organises special walks for the Bloomsday festival and also runs regular Joycean walks.

Dalkey Castle & Heritage Centre www.dalkeycastle.com celebrates Bloomsday with a walk past places connected with Joyce in the area and with a Joycean Evening involving performances from his work.

Michael Judge
1921-

Born in Drumcondra, Michael Judge is a playwright, short story writer and writer for radio and television. Although he worked as a full-time teacher and toward the end of his teaching career was Vice Principal of Coláiste Mhuire in Dublin, from the 1950s on he was also a regular contributor to RTÉ, writing his own radio plays as well as writing scripts for well-known radio and television series including *Tolka Row*, *Harbour Hotel*, *Wanderly Wagon*, *The Riordans* and *Glenroe*. He published his first novel, *Vintage Red*, in 2004 at the age of 83. A second novel followed in 2005, *From The Left Hand*.

Patrick Kavanagh
1904-67

Never quite comfortable here, yet never happy to return to the 'stony grey soil' from which he came in Inniskeen, County Monaghan, poet Patrick Kavanagh is just one of the many writers who came to Dublin and, although they moved away, just kept coming back. The son of a small farmer-cum-cobbler, he left school at thirteen and worked alongside his father. However the call of the pen was strong and he began to write and submit poetry to newspapers and journals. He had some success, with the *Dundalk Democrat* and the *Irish Independent*, but it was AE who gave him his real start by publishing three of his poems –

Kavanagh statue by the Grand Canal at Mespil Road

The Intangible, *Dreamer* and *Ploughman* while he was editor at the *Irish Statesman*. Kavanagh actually walked the 80km from Monaghan to Dublin to meet him and had the added bonus of being introduced to Frank O'Connor, and the poet James Sullivan Starkey, (Seumas O'Sullivan). Eleven years later he moved to Dublin, then spent some time in Belfast before finally settling in Dublin.

He never seemed to put down roots anywhere for long. He had numerous addresses, from Drumcondra to 33 Haddington Road, which he shared with his brother Peter, before they moved to 122 Morehampton Road, then Percy Place, and then to 9 O'Connell Street. They parted company at this stage and Patrick relocated to 62 Pembroke Road for his longest sojourn anywhere. Then came Raglan Road, a place he immortalised in his poem of the same name. Later he moved again, to 110 Baggot Street, 1 Wilton Place, 37 Upper Mount Street, the Halcyon Hotel in South Anne Street and his final home at 136 Upper Leeson Street.

He and his brother started a newspaper called *Kavanagh's Weekly* in 1952, but it closed down after 13 editions, due, in Kavanagh's words, 'to the quality of the audience.'

He was a well-known figure walking alongside the canal and is remembered for his curmudgeonly expression and unkempt appearance. Much of his social life revolved around the pub and pint culture, where something of a literary revival of its own was happening in the snugs and on the barstools of Searsons, Mooney's and the Waterloo in Baggot Street, the Palace Bar in Fleet Street, Neary's in Chatham Street, McDaid's in Harry Street and in The Bailey in Duke Street.

Kavanagh's autobiography, *The Green Fool*, resulted in his being sued for libel by Oliver St John Gogarty. He came to notoriety again when he published his poem, *The Great Hunger*, in *The Horizon* literary magazine. This was seized under an order from the Minister for Justice who deemed it to be unfit for the delicate and moral minds of the time. Ironically, he was given a job writing for the *Standard*, the Catholic paper, on the recommendation of Archbishop of Dublin, John Charles McQuaid. Kavanagh wrote under a pseudonym, Piers Plowman, in the *Irish Press*, where he was also a film critic. He was a regular at Parsons bookshop and newsagents on Baggot Street Bridge, a venue for the literati in

Dublin at the time. It closed down in 1989. There is a Patrick Kavanagh Centre beside St Mary's Church at Inniskeen, close to where he is buried. The annual Patrick Kavanagh Poetry Award is given for a collection of unpublished poems and a Patrick Kavanagh Weekend takes place on the last weekend of November each year in Inniskeen, around the anniversary of his death.

Kavanagh's *Raglan Road* was set to the music of a traditional ballad and has been recorded by numerous artists, including Luke Kelly and Sinead O'Connor.

At Downtown Disney in Orlando there is a statue of Kavanagh outside a pub called Raglan Road. In Dublin two benches commemorate him: one depicts Kavanagh sitting in contemplative mood by the Grand Canal at Mespil Road. The other, a simple bench of wood and stone, erected by friends who knew how he loved this spot, is on the opposite bank at the lock gates by Baggot Street Bridge. It was unveiled on St Patrick's Day 1968 and each year on that day followers gather to remember him and his *Lines Written on a Seat on the Grand Canal in Dublin.*

'O commemorate me where there is water,

Canal water preferably,
Greeny at the heart of summer.
Brother…
Commemorate me thus
beautifully.'

Peadar Kearney
1888-1942

Peadar Kearney, who was born at 68 Dorset Street, wrote the words to the Irish national anthem, *The Soldier's Song* or *Amhrán na bhFiann*. He was the uncle of the Behan brothers and, like Brendan, was a house painter, although he also worked as a stagehand at the Abbey Theatre. He had many addresses around the city during his life, including Marino, Summerhill, 49 Dolphin's Barn Street, 10 Lower Dominick Street, Russell Place and 3 Richmond Parade, both off the North Circular Road and finally at 25 O'Donoghue Street, Inchicore. He is buried in the Republican plot in Glasnevin Cemetery.

'But the Angelus Bell o'er the Liffey swell rang out through the foggy dew' –The Foggy Dew, words written by Peadar Kearney

Thomas Kettle
1880-1916

Journalist, poet and writer Thomas 'Tom' Kettle was born in Artane, Dublin. He had his primary school education with the Christian Brothers in North Richmond Street, where he met Oliver St John Gogarty, who was two years his senior. They were both boarders at Clongowes Wood in County Kildare, where they shared a passion for cycling and started a lasting friendship. Kettle was a star pupil, quickly getting a name for himself on the debating team and for his witty prose. At University College Dublin he shone as an orator and was elected as successor to Francis Skeffington as the auditor of the Literary and Historical Society. He used to attend Sunday evening salons at the Sheehy house at 2 Belvedere Place with James Joyce and Oliver St John Gogarty. There he met Mary Sheehy, sister of Hanna Sheehy Skeffington, and they married in 1907, in St Mary's Pro-Cathedral.

On receiving a BA in Mental and Moral Science, he decided to read Law at the King's Inns in Henrietta Street. His interest in politics was ever growing and he joined The Young Ireland Branch of the United Irish League, and became its first President. He also became editor of *The Nationist*, an unconventional weekly that championed such topics as women's suffrage and the Irish literary revival. He resigned following controversy over an allegedly anti-clerical article. Shortly after that he became MP for East Tyrone and represented the constituency for four years. He went on to pursue other avenues and shortly afterwards his books, *Home Rule Finance* and *The Open Secret of Ireland* were published.

He served as a war correspondent during WWI, having gone to Belgium initially with the British Army. He then joined the Royal Dublin Fusiliers and after the executions following the Easter Rising, he volunteered for active duties and was dispatched to France in July 1916. He was killed on 9 September 1916, one of the thousands who perished in the battle of the Somme. His body was never recovered but he is remembered with a monument in St Stephen's Green (*see photo*), inscribed with some lines from a sonnet he had written for his little daughter Betty, only days before he died. These read:

THOMAS M KETTLE
1880-1916
Born-County Dublin
17 February 1880
Killed at Guinchy
9th September 1916
Poet, Essayist, Patriot

Died not for flag, nor king, nor emperor, but for a dream, born in a herdsman's hut, and for the secret scripture of the poor.

Kettle's other works include *Poems and Parodies, Irish Orators and Oratory. Battle Songs of the Irish Brigades, To My Daughter Betty - The Gift of God.* His book *The Ways of War,* reasons for serving in WWI, was published posthumously in 1917.

Marian Keyes
1963-

Limerick-born Marian Keyes was raised in Monkstown and now lives in Dun Laoghaire. She is one of the most successful of the current wave of popular writers of women's fiction. A unifying thread in all her novels is the struggle to escape the real hells of addiction, loss, domestic violence and depression – themes she mixes with comedic relief and happy-ever-after solutions. *Watermelon,* her first novel was published in 1995. She has since written eleven. *The Other Side of the Story* was the second highest selling novel in 2005, and this

Marian Keyes and Cathy Kelly

achievement was repeated two years later with *Anybody Out There* and surpassed in 2009 by *This Charming Man. Watermelon* was made into a movie. *Rachel's Holiday* is currently in production starring Katherine Zeta Jones, and *Lucy Sullivan is Getting Married* was made into a sixteen-part television series.

Declan Kiberd
1951-

Professor Declan Kiberd had a good start in life when he was taught at Belgrove Boys School in Clontarf by none other than writer John McGahern. He progressed to St Paul's College Raheny, before making his name as a brilliant scholar at Trinity College. His career has seen him become Chair of Anglo-Irish Literature and Drama at UCD. He also taught Irish at Trinity College. On the literary front his *Inventing Ireland: the literature of modern Ireland,* is considered by many to be his major work. He has also written *Men and Feminism, Irish Classics, Ulysses and Us* and *Idir Dhá Chultúr.*

TRINITY ALUMNI

Throughout the centuries many of Dublin's literati attended Trinity College or The University of Dublin. Some of these include the ever-quotable:

Jonathan Swift – *A man should never be ashamed to own that he has been in the wrong, which is but saying ... that he is wiser today than yesterday.*

William Congreve – *Music has charms to soothe a savage breast.*

George Berkeley – *He who says there is no such thing as an honest man, you may be sure is himself a knave.*

Oliver Goldsmith – *Ceremonies are different in every country, but true politeness is everywhere the same.*

Edmund Burke – *If we command our wealth, we shall be rich and free; if our wealth commands us, we are poor indeed.*

JM Synge – *In a good play every speech should be as fully flavoured as a nut or apple.*

Oscar Wilde – *One should never trust a woman who tells one her real age. A woman who would tell one that, would tell one anything*

Samuel Beckett – *We are all born mad. Some remain so.*

J P Donleavy – *When you don't have any money the problem is food. When you have money it's sex. When you have both it's health.*

Among the other well-known literary names who attended Trinity College are:

Charles Robert Maturin
Joseph Sheridan Le Fanu
Bram Stoker
Percy French
Douglas Hyde
Samuel Beckett
William Trevor
Sebastian Barry
Eoin Colfer
John Boyne
Anne Enright
Derek Mahon
Patrick Longley
Eavan Boland

Patrick MacDonogh
Oliver St. John Gogarty
Michael Hartnett

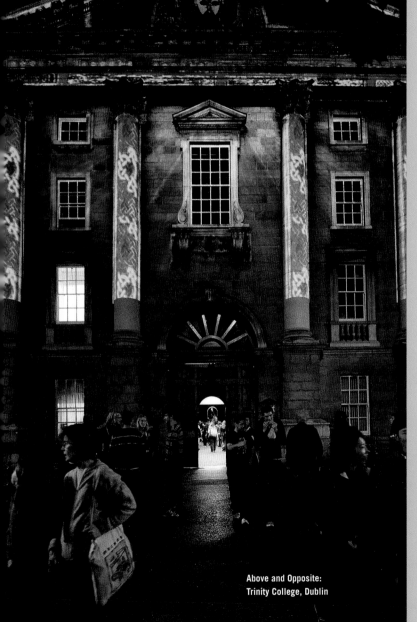

Above and Opposite:
Trinity College, Dublin

Charles J Kickham
1828-82

Charles Kickham was born in Mullinahone, Co Tipperary and was greatly affected by the political atmosphere of his times. He wrote ten novels, all endorsing the nationalist cause. These include *Sally Cavanagh*, which he dedicated to John O'Leary and *Knocknagow*, effectively an attack on the land tenure system. He also wrote the words of the song *Slievenamon*. He contributed to the *Nation*, the *Irishman* and the *Celt*.

In 1865 he was arrested with James Stephens and charged for writing 'treasonous' articles and for committing high treason. He was sentenced to fourteen years penal servitude. On his release in 1869 he went back to Tipperary, but later returned to Dublin. He spent some time at 2 Montpelier Place, Stradbrook Road in Blackrock, staying with friends. In poor health and almost blind from an explosion when he was 13, he was run down by a jaunting cart at College Green and sustained a broken leg. Two years later, at just fifty-four, he had a stroke that killed him. His wish had been to be buried in his beloved Mullinahone. The funeral procession taking his coffin to the train at Kingsbridge Station, (now Heuston) was accompanied by eleven bands

and thousands of mourners. He is buried in St Michael's churchyard. The inscription on his headstone reads

...journalist, novelist, poet but before all, patriot, traitor to crime, vice, fraud but true to Ireland and to God.

A second stone 'dedicated by the people of Mullinahone and other friends' was placed on his grave in 1950.

Benedict Kiely
1919-2007

The mellifluous voice of Benedict 'Ben' Kiely wafted through many homes over the years as he broadcast his observations and witticisms on *The Humours of Donnybrook* and *Sunday Miscellany*. He came to Dublin, albeit taking a circuitous route, from his homeland of Tyrone. That journey saw him go from post office clerk to a period in Emo, Portarlington, when he'd decided he wanted to become a Jesuit. A tubercular spinal ailment put paid to that plan and he spent a prolonged stay in recovery at Cappagh Hospital in Finglas, during which he decided to go to UCD. While there he wrote for the *Weekly Standard*, to which Patrick Kavanagh was also a contributor. Once qualified in History and Letters, he began working for the

Irish Independent and after five years joined the *Irish Press* as a literary editor. He held that position for fourteen years before going to the US, where he took up writer-in-residence at various universities before coming back to Dublin. In a career that spanned six decades his writings garnered for him much acclaim and many accolades. He was given the Award for Literature from the Irish Academy of Letters and in 1996 he was made a Saoi of Aosdána.

Although he was sixty-nine years out of Tyrone when he died, he is fondly remembered there and now honoured annually in Omagh with the Benedict Kiely Literary Weekend.

He wrote an autobiography, *Drink to the Bird: An Omagh Boyhood*; *The Waves Behind Us: A Memoir*, and *Poor Scholar: A Study of the Works and Days of William Carleton 1794-1869* as well as fourteen novels, (the first three of which were banned!) and numerous non-fiction works and short stories. His funeral Mass was held in Donnybrook, close to where he had lived and supped happily in the local hostelries, holding impromptu court and captivating listeners and friends. He is buried in Omagh.

Thomas Kinsella
1928-

Poet Thomas Kinsella was born in Inchicore and educated at the local Model School and O'Connell Christian Brothers School before going to UCD, initially by day and then as a night student after he joined the civil service. While at college he contributed to *Poetry Ireland* and *The National Student*. His works include *Poems*, *Another September*, *Moralities* and *Nightwalker*.

In 2007 Kinsella was made an Honorary Freeman of the City of Dublin.

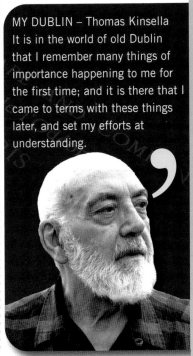

MY DUBLIN – Thomas Kinsella
It is in the world of old Dublin that I remember many things of importance happening to me for the first time; and it is there that I came to terms with these things later, and set my efforts at understanding.

Dick King by Thomas Kinsella from
A Dublin Documentary (The O'Brien Press, Dublin, 2006)

In your ghost, Dick King, in your phantom vowels I read
That death roves our memories igniting
Love. Kind plague, low voice in a stubbled throat,
You haunt with the taint of age and of vanished good,
Fouling my thought with losses.

Clearly now I remember rain on the cobbles,
Ripples in the iron trough, and the horses' dipped
Faces under the Fountain in James's Street,
When I sheltered my nine years against your buttons
And your own dread years were to come:

And your voice, in a pause of softness, named the dead,
Hushed as though the city had died by fire,
Bemused, discovering ... discovering
A gate to enter temperate ghosthood by;
And I squeezed your fingers till you found
My hand hidden in yours.

Claire Kilroy
1973-

Novelist Claire Kilroy is a Dubliner
whose book *All Summer* won the
2004 Rooney Prize for Irish
Literature. It was also shortlisted for
the 2004 Kerry Group Irish Fiction
Award. Other titles include
Tenderwire and *All Names Have
Been Changed*.

Thomas Kilroy
1934-

The Kilkenny-born playwright and
novelist studied at University
College, Dublin and was play editor
in the Abbey Theatre for a period.
He was Professor of English in UCG
but resigned in 1989 to concentrate
on his writing. Since then he has
written numerous plays and won
many awards, including a Lifetime

Achievement Awards Irish Times/ESB in 2004. His novel, *The Big Chapel*, was awarded the Guardian Fiction Prize, 1971 and was shortlisted for the Booker Prize. He is a member of the Irish Academy of Letters, the Royal Society of Literature and Aosdána.

Maura Laverty
1907-66

Maura Laverty, journalist, cookery writer and novelist, came to live in Dublin following a period as a governess and journalist in Spain. After her marriage she lived in Fitzwilliam Square. Her second novel *Touched by the Thorn* won the Irish Women Writers Award in 1943, but it was banned for its immoral content – its married heroine was unfaithful. However it's her *Lift Up Your Gates* novel that puts Laverty here among these other writers. This reveals the story of Chrissie, a slum child who lived with her family in one room in Westland Row, in a city of squalor and sickness, unemployment and want. It was marketed as *Liffey Lane* in America and adapted by RTÉ as *Tolka Row*, the station's first soap opera, where it ran for four years. She is buried in Glasnevin Cemetery.

Mary Lavin
1912-96

Mary Lavin was born in Massachusetts, but her family returned to Ireland, to Galway initially and, when she was ten, to settle in Dublin, where she attended Loreto College on St Stephen's Green. Following her time in UCD she became a French teacher in her former school. Her work, much of it award-winning, includes twenty books, short stories, novellas and children's books. Her only two novels were *The House on Clewe Street* and *Mary O'Grady*. She wasn't afraid to tackle thorny subjects and dealt with many feminist issues as well as the abuses in institutions that were run by state and church.

She was given an honorary doctorate from UCD and from 1964 to 1965 served as President of Irish PEN. She also served as President of the Irish Academy of Letters from 1971-1973 and was a member of Aosdána, made a Saoi in 1992.

She was married twice, having met the two men when in UCD. Both her husbands predeceased her, but they are all buried in a family plot in St Mary's Cemetery, Navan, County Meath.

Hugh Leonard
1926-2009

The dramatist, writer and columnist assumed the name Hugh Leonard, but he was known to close friends as Jack and to others as John Keyes Byrne. He was a well-known figure around Dalkey where he grew up and lived for most of his life, apart from some years in Manchester. He went to Harold Boys' National School from where he won a scholarship to the Presentation College in Glasthule. He then joined the civil service. He began writing and produced at least eighteen plays, two volumes of essays, one novel, *Parnell and the Englishwoman*, numerous screen and teleplays including the adaptation of James Plunkett's *Strumpet City* for RTÉ. He also wrote two autobiographies *Home Before Night* and *Out after Dark*. He set his highly successful play *Da* in the environs of Dalkey, amid the ghosts of his childhood there. This won a Tony Award and was later made into a film starring Martin Sheen and Barnard Hughes

I'm a writer, and what I do is write. I wasn't able to do anything else-

Hugh Leonard

Charles Lever
1806-72

Often described as the Irish Dickens, this medical doctor published over thirty titles in his lifetime, and five volumes of essays. Born in 34 Amiens Street when this area contained fashionable residences, Charles went to several schools, including Mr Ford's on Amiens Street and the Proprietary School at 2 Great Denmark Street run by a Rev. Wright. While still at school he was smitten with a girl who lived at Sir John Rogerson's Quay. *The Life of Charles Lever* (1905) by W J Fitzpatrick, reports,

'Charlie was attracted by a pretty little girl who lived in the Marine School, and thither he used to steal to get a sight of or a word with her almost daily. One of his acquaintances was in the habit of supplying him with flowers, which were sometimes given by the boy-lover to the girl ...'

The girl, Kate Baker, later became his wife. Their romance featured in a book *Famous Love Matches* by Catherine Jane Hamilton (1908), although the marriage, in 1833, did not have her father's approval. Lever was a wild student at Trinity College, where he roomed in 2 Botany Bay. He took some took time out and went to Canada on an emigrant ship, toured in Holland and Germany, before returning to further his medical courses in Sir Patrick Dun's Hospital on Grand Canal Street. He then went to Dr Steeven's Hospital in Steeven's Lane, where Lever and William Wilde, Oscar's father, were contemporaries. Neither establishment functions as a hospital today. After he qualified, Lever practiced in Clare and Derry before returning to Dublin. When his parents died, he was left a wealthy man, but a gambling habit made inroads on his finances and prompted him to write. His first novel, *The Confessions of Harry Lorrequer*, was serialised in the *Dublin University Magazine*. This was followed by *Charles O'Malley: the Irish Dragoon*, an adventure-packed Victorian military novel that made his name as a writer. He moved to Brussels for a period and gave up medicine in favour of writing.

On his return to Dublin he became the editor of the *Dublin University Magazine*. He lived in Stillorgan and Dun Laoghaire before moving to Templeogue House, where his children had horses called after characters in his novels. There he entertained William Makepeace Thackeray on his grand tour of Ireland and who dedicated his *Irish Sketch Book* to him.

Lever left Ireland for good in 1845. He was appointed British Vice-Consul in La Spezia in Italy by Lord Derby who is reputed to have declared '*£600 a year for doing nothing, and you, Lever, are just the man to do it*'. He was later elevated to Consul in Trieste, where he died and is buried in the British Cemetery. His headstone bears the inscription in English: *Charles Lever, Born near Dublin 31 August 1809 Died at Trieste 1 June 1872.*

His diaries for 1828-29 are held in the RIA in Dublin.

THACKERAY'S IMPRESSIONS OF DUBLIN, 1845
William Makepeace Thackeray observed: '*The street is exceedingly broad and handsome; the shops at the commencement, rich and spacious; but in Upper Sackville Street, which closes with the pretty building and gardens of the Rotunda, the appearance of wealth begins to fade somewhat, and the houses look as if they had seen better days. Even in this, the great street of the town, there is scarcely any one, and it is as vacant and listless as Pall Mall in October.*'

Morgan Llywelyn
1937-

This American-born author, who has become an Irish citizen and lives in County Dublin, is best known for her historical fiction, historical fantasy, and historical non-fiction. She has received many awards and her books have sold over 40 million copies worldwide. In 1999 she received the *Exceptional Celtic Woman of the Year Award* from Celtic Women International. This is given 'to honour, celebrate and promote Celtic women and their heritage' Her novels include *Lion of Ireland, O'Sullivan's March, Grania;She-king of the Irish Seas, Pride of Lions* and *Brendan –The remarkable Life and Voyage of Brendan of Clonfert*. She has also written historical fiction for young readers, including *Pirate Queen, Strongbow* and *The Young Rebels*.

Lord Longford
1902-61

Edward Pakenham, 6th Earl of Longford, was a playwright and the saviour of the Gate Theatre (*see photo, centre*). He became a director of the theatre three years after its foundation in 1931. He also invested heavily in it when he formed Longford Productions, his own company, which rented the theatre for six months every year and took it touring around Ireland. He also rescued it in 1956 when it was threatened with demolition by Dublin Corporation. During his involvement, with which his novelist and playwright wife Christine collaborated, he translated many works from French, Greek and Irish, including Merriman's *Cúirt an Mheán Oíche – the Midnight Court*. His own works include *Yahoo, The Medians, The Dove in the Castle* and the *Vineyard*. He was a member of the Irish Senate (Seanad) between 1946 and 1948.

Lady Longford
1900-80

nee Christine Trew, lived with her husband Lord Longford in Grosvenor

Park, 123 Leinster Road, Rathmines. She wrote *Mr Jiggins of Jigginstown*, *Printed Cotton* and *Making Conversations*. They are both buried in Mount Jerome Cemetery, Harold's Cross and their gravestone has the symbolic masks of tragedy and comedy on either side.

Samuel Lover
1797-1868

Writer, painter and novelist Samuel Lover was an accomplished gentleman who was born at 60 Grafton Street. He was a member of the Royal Hibernian Academy to which he submitted countless miniatures – all the rage in those days – as well as landscapes and drawings. At the same time he was writing songs and contributing to the *Dublin Literary Gazette*, to which he submitted his ballad, Rory O'More. This was later turned into a novel and a play. He married and lived at 9 D'Olier Street for a time before moving to London in 1935. While there he wrote his best-known novel *Handy Andy*, which was credited with being 'a pill to purge melancholy'. He worked on *Bentley's Miscellany* with Charles Dickens who was its first editor and started *Irish Evenings*, entertainments which proved to be a great social success

He is buried in Kensal Green, London, although he died in Jersey. He is remembered in his hometown of Dublin with a plaque in St Patrick's Cathedral. This reads:

'In memory of Samuel Lover, Poet, Painter, Novelist and Composer, who in the exercise of a genius as distinguished in its versatility as in its power, by the pen and pencil illustrated so happily the characteristics of the Peasantry of his country that his name will ever be honourably identified with Ireland.'

Patricia Lynch
1894-1972

Patricia Lynch is best known for her children's literature and especially for *The Turf-Cutter's Donkey*. She wrote some forty-eight novels and two hundred short stories.

Born in Cork, she received her education at schools in Ireland, England, Scotland and Belgium. As a journalist she was sent to Dublin by Sylvia Pankhurst to report on the Easter Rising for *The Workers' Dreadnought*. She married socialist historian R M Fox in Dublin and they settled in Glasnevin. She died in Monkstown and is buried in Glasnevin Cemetery with her husband. Her semi-autobiographical *A Story-Teller's Childhood* was published in 1947.

Detail of Desmond Kinney's 1974 mosaic mural, Setanta Wall, also known as the Táin Wall, off Nassau Street. It depicts scenes from the epic saga of The Táin

James Joyce gazes across at the GPO from his position on North Earl Street

Key to Route 1: Dublin Writers' Museum to O'Connell Street

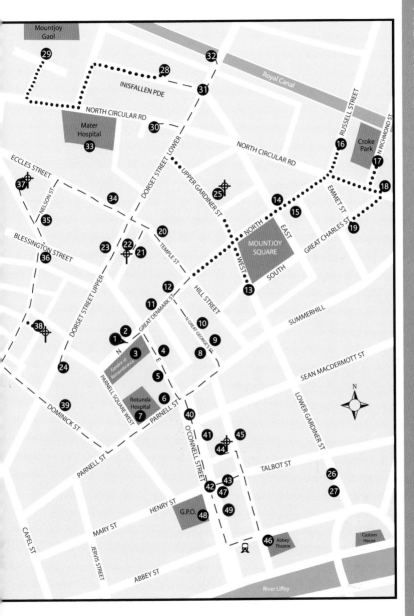

Walking route 1:
Dublin Writers' Museum to O'Connell Street

It seems fitting that any literary walk in Dublin should begin at the **Dublin Writers' Museum (1)** in Dublin 1. Apart from the museum itself many of the writers at the end of the 19th and beginning of the 20th centuries were born in the immediate vicinity. Dublin postal districts 1 and 7 (the odd numbers in our city refer to those on north of the Liffey; the even ones are south of it) were then considered highly desirable addresses. The houses were impressive homes with many inhabited by important personages in this highly fashionable quarter of Dublin.

You'll find the Writers' Museum at **18 Parnell Street North**, right next door to the **Irish Writers' Centre at number 19 (2)**, which nurtures emerging talent and fosters relationships between writers and their Irish audiences. These two venues overlook **The Garden of Remembrance (3)**, the city park that is dedicated to the men and women who died in pursuit of Irish freedom. Several leaders of the 1916 Easter Rising were held overnight here before being taken to Kilmainham Gaol. In 1976 a contest was held to find a poem that would express the appreciation and the inspiration of the struggle for freedom and it was won by the Dublin-born author Liam Mac Uistin, whose poem *We Saw a Vision* is written in Irish, English and French on the wall of the monument.

Turn right into **Parnell Square East** where **number 5 (4)**, on your left, is the birthplace of Oliver St John Gogarty. This used to be called Rutland Square, but was changed, like many of Dublin's place names, when Ireland got her independence, to honour Irish heroes and patriots.

Continue down into **Cavendish Row**, home to the famous **Gate Theatre (5)**, established as a theatre in 1930 by Hilton Edwards and Micheál MacLiammóir. It was here that Orson Welles, James Mason, Geraldine FitzGerald and Michael Gambon began their acting careers.

Turn right into Parnell Street. The **Rotunda Rooms (6)** was a popular auditorium where Cardinal John Henry Newman lectured in 1852. He was the founder of The Literary and Historical Society at the newly established Catholic University of Ireland, now UCD. The Rotunda Rooms were also the venue where Charles Dickens gave public readings on his visits in 1858 and 1867.

The block to the right that goes around into Parnell Sq West is almost totally taken over by the

Rotunda Hospital (7), the first maternity hospital in the world and the place where Christy Brown, Brian Desmond Behan and John Betjeman's daughter, Candida, were born. It also features in Roddy Doyle's award-winning book *The Snapper*.

Go left along Parnell Street then take a left into **North Great George's Street** where **number 20 (8)** was affectionately referred to as The Ferguson Arms because of the legendary hospitality of its owner, poet Samuel Ferguson, who regularly entertained Sheridan Le Fanu, Lady Morgan, Charles James Lever and others there. **Number 35** now houses the **James Joyce Centre (9)**, a mecca for Joycean followers (*see* Venues, page 206). It was once the studio of Denis Maginni – the Professor of Dancing who appears in *Ulysses*. **Number 38 (10)** was one of the residences of John Pentland Mahaffy who was Oscar Wilde's tutor in the art of conversation at Trinity College. Number 44 (since rebuilt) was where Lady Morgan's father died. He was Robert Owenson who bought the Musik Theatre in Fishamble Street, where Handel's Messiah was first performed.

Continue to the junction with **Great Denmark Street**. On your left, number 2 (11) was formerly a school attended by novelist Charles Lever. Now the street is dominated by the Jesuit boys' school, **Belvedere College (12)**, whose literary alumni include Austin Clarke, Joseph Mary Plunkett, James Joyce, Tim Pat Coogan and Mervyn Wall.

Proceed right to the junction with Hill St/Temple St.

Diversion: An interesting detour at this stage would be to continue straight into Gardiner Place and on to **Mountjoy Square**. *John O'Leary and WB Yeats were lodgers at* **number 53 (13)** *on the west side of the square, to your right, while Sean O'Casey lived in a now demolished house at* **35 Mountjoy Square South**, *purported to be the setting for his play,* The Shadow of a Gunman. *From Mountjoy Square North continue into Belvedere Place, where James Joyce was regularly a guest at the home of the Sheehys at* **number 2 Belvedere Place (14)**; *their daughter married poet Thomas Kettle.*

Number 14 (now **34**) **Fitzgibbon Street (15)** *was one of the numerous addresses of the Joyce family throughout the city. If you go to the end of this street and cross over the North Circular Road you are almost facing Russell*

Street where Brendan Behan's grandmother had property and where the young Behan grew up at *14 Russell Street*. The **Behan Square apartment (16)** complex has replaced these houses.

Double back here to the **North Circular Road** and turn left. The next left will bring you to another Joyce abode, at *17 North Richmond Street (17)*, just across from the Christian Brothers School that Joyce attended. So too did his friends Gogarty and Kettle. Back on **North Circular Road**, and to your left, numbers *609* and *617 (18)* (then 17 and 21 Richmond Place) were where Joyce lived when he returned to Dublin in 1912 during his protracted dispute with his publisher George Roberts over his book Dubliners. James Clarence Mangan worked in the Ordnance Survey Offices at *21 Great Charles Street (19)*, where artist George Petrie lived for fifteen years.

Back to the main route! Take a left into **Temple Street**, where bibliophile and journalist John O'Leary lived at the now demolished **number 17**. Fanny Parnell, sister of Charles Stewart Parnell, resided at 14, now part of **Temple Street Hospital (20)**. She was a regular poetry contributor to the *Irish People*.

A short distance up Temple St,

take a left onto **Hardwicke Place** where you'll find **number 4, Waverley House (21)**, which was the setting of Joyce's 'The Boarding House' in *Dubliners*. The Joyce family lived at 29, which no longer stands. Facing this is the deconsecrated **St George's Church (22)**. It was the bells from here that Bloom could hear pealing in Ulysses. They now ring out from Taney Parish Church in Dundrum. The church became a nightclub and then briefly the Temple Theatre in 2002, but it closed shortly afterwards. There was another theatre in Hardwicke Place previously, The Irish Theatre, founded by Edward Martyn, Thomas MacDonagh and Joseph Plunkett.

Retrace your steps to Temple Street and continue along to the junction with Dorset Street. If you take a **left** here you will come to **number 85 (23)** on **Upper Dorset Street**, where Sean O'Casey was born, while Richard Brinsley Sheridan's home was further down at **number 12 (24)**. Alternatively, take a **right** at the Temple St junction into Dorset Street Lower.

*Diversion: About halfway along here take a right into **Upper Gardiner Street** for a quick look at St **Francis Xavier's Church (25)**. This church was the one from which Gerard Manley Hopkins' funeral took place. It was also where he attended Mass* *when he lodged in Upper Gardiner Street. **Note**: You can, if you wish, continue on down to Lower Gardiner Street where Dion Boucicault was born at **number 47(26)**. **Number 48 (27)** was where Lafcadio Hearn spent some of his boyhood in Dublin. However, this will bring you almost back to the city centre and quite a long way from the northern part of the main route.*

If you are continuing on the main route, walk back from the church **(25)** and continue along Lower Dorset Street, crossing over the North Circular Road. The next left is **Innisfallen Parade**. **No 9 (28)** is the single story house occupied by Sean O'Casey's family after his father had sustained a spinal injury. This street is close to Glengariff Parade, another of the Joyce abodes.

*Diversion: These low-rise houses are shadowed by **Mountjoy Gaol (29)**, where Brendan Behan set* The Quare Fella, *Other 'guests' here were Charles J Kickham, Maud Gonne, Peadar O'Donnell and Mannix Flynn.*

Back on **North Circular Road**, Sean O'Casey lived at **422 (30)**, where he is said to have written his best plays. By doubling back here you'll go into **Dorset Street** where Peadar Kearney, author of

the words to the Irish national anthem *Amhrán na bhFiann*, or *the Soldier's Song*, was born at **number 68 (31)**. He was an uncle of the Behan brothers. Further along Dorset Street, away from the city at the Royal Canal junction with Whitworth Road, you'll find a **statue** of his nephew, **Brendan Behan (32)**, sitting on a park bench.

Going back down Dorset Street towards the city centre, turn right into **Eccles Street**, home of the Dominican Convent where novelist Patricia Scanlan and Val Mulkerns, a tireless campaigner against censorship, went to school. The Dominican Convent and many of the houses around here have been subsumed into the **Mater Hospital (33)** complex. However, this street featured in Behan's *The Hostage*. In *Ulysses* Leopold Bloom lived at **number 7 Eccles Street (34)**. Turning left into Nelson Street will bring you to **number 2 (35)**, where Joseph Sheridan Le Fanu lived with his wife Susan Bennett after their marriage in 1844. This leads into **Blessington Street** where Iris Murdoch was born in **number 15 (36)**. (**Berkeley Road Church (37)** is close by, on Berkeley Street, behind and to your right - this was where Austin Clarke's family attended weekly Mass.) Continue down Mountjoy Street where the Clarke family lived at **number 15**.

*Diversion: On your left is St Mary's Place, the location of **St Mary's Church (38)** or the 'Black Church' and of the Christian Brothers School that Austin Clarke attended. He was fascinated by the legend associated with the church that anybody who walked anti-clockwise around it at midnight with one eye closed, would meet the devil! He never tried it, though.*

Proceed down Mountjoy Street to the junction with Dominick Street. Turn left into Dominick Street, where Miss Sydney Owenson, later Lady Morgan, was a governess to the Featherstonhaughs and Austin Clarke attended the Holy Faith Convent School. Sheridan Le Fanu was born at number 45, but this building has long since been demolished, and O'Casey lived with his widowed mother and sister in the top floor flat at number **20, Lower Dominick Street (39)**, where he also attended St Mary's Infant School downstairs, before progressing to the national school on the same street.

Go to the end of Dominick Street and turn left into Parnell Street, walk along by the Rotunda Hospital on your left and you'll see the tall **Parnell monument (40)** ahead on a traffic island. Turn right here and you're in **O'Connell Street**, formerly Sackville Street. On your left you'll spot the **Gresham Hotel (41)** where Maud Gonne used to stay on her visits to Dublin and when she attended the Gate Theatre. Continue down towards the River Liffey and you'll come to a major intersection, dissected by the **Spire (42)**. If you turn left here into North Earl Street, a very short distance down you'll see a statue of **James Joyce (43)**. Dubliners tend to nickname their statues as soon as they are installed. This is known as *The Prick with the Stick*. Continue to the next crossroads. If you take a left here on to Marlborough Street, and the next left, you'll see the **Pro-Cathedral (44)** where the Palestrina Choir, started by Edward Martyn, is based. On the opposite side of the road, in the grounds of the **Department of Education (45)** are the buildings of the Model School attended by Sean O'Casey and George Bernard Shaw. Double back on to Marlborough Street and continue past the junction with Talbot Street. The next junction is with Lower Abbey Street where you'll see the **Abbey Theatre (46)** on the corner. **The Peacock** is also housed here, the more innovative and experimental side of the National Theatre of Ireland,

providing an official stage for emerging Irish writers and theatre companies. Take a right up Abbey Street and you're in O'Connell Street again. Take a right: Percy Bysshe Shelley stayed at lodgings at **number 7 Lower Sackville Street (47)**. On the opposite side is the **General Post Office (GPO) (48)** where the Easter Rising took place in 1916. Among those in the building holding out against the British were poets Patrick Pearse, Joseph Mary Plunkett and Thomas MacDonagh. Denis Florence McCarthy's home was just across from the GPO and was later to become the Imperial Hotel, which was destroyed by fire in the 1916 disturbances. The whole block was rebuilt and **Clery's Department Store (49)** now occupies the site.

Above: One of Robin Buick's pavement plaques marking places on the *Ulysses* trail.
Below: The Dublin Writers Museum

(plaque text) ULYSSES STYLE. 'AEOLUS - the offices of the Evening Telegraph (*Ulysses*, Episode 7)'. C&C Proudly Sponsored by Cantrell & Cochrane (Dublin) Limited

(building sign) DUBLIN WRITERS MUSEUM

The Walks:2

St Patrick's Cathedral to Westland Row

The Literary Parade in St Patrick's Park. Behind the grilles are plaques commemorating well-known Dublin writers.

THIS BRONZE COMMEMORATES
THE FIRST PERFORMANCE OF
GEORGE FRIDERIC HANDEL'S
ORATORIO MESSIAH GIVEN
IN THE OLD MUSICK HALL
FISHAMBLE STREET DUBLIN
ON TUESDAY

JOYCE

DUBLINERS
ULYSSES
FINNEGANS WAKE

CLARKE

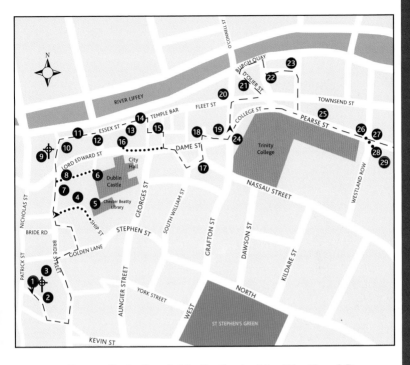

Key to Route 2: St Patrick's Cathedral to Westland Row

1 St Patrick's Cathedral
2 Marsh's Library
3 St Patrick's Park/Literary Parade
4 Hoey's Court
5 Chester Beatty Library
6 Dublin Castle
7 St Werburgh's Church
8 The Bull & Castle
9 Christ Church Cathedral
10 Fishamble Street
11 Smock Alley
12 12 Parliament Street
13 The New Theatre
14 Temple Bar Culture Box
15 Cecelia House
16 Olympia Theatre

17 Dublin Tourism (St Andrew's Church)
18 Foster Place/Wax Museum
19 Bank of Ireland
20 The Palace Bar
21 9 D'Olier Street
22 Hawkin's Street
23 Mulligan's Pub
24 Trinity College
25 27 Pearse Street (the Pearse House)
26 St Mark's Church
27 52 Pearse Street (The Academy)
28 Church of St Andrew (Westland Row Church)
29 Christian Brothers School

Walking route 2:
St Patrick's Cathedral to
Westland Row

This walking route brings you around old Dublin, the Dublin where Swift and his contemporaries walked and wrote.

Let's begin at **St Patrick's Cathedral (1)**. St Patrick baptised converts at a well adjacent to the site, so when they built the original church they dedicated it to him. Centuries later, in 1220, the present church was built. It was a Roman Catholic place of worship until Oliver Cromwell's rule. He stabled his horses in the nave.

Jonathan Swift became dean of the cathedral in 1713 and nowadays his name is synonymous with this place. The cathedral is well worth a visit, so let's go inside.

The cathedral is the final resting place for many well-known names including Swift himself and his Stella, who lies beside him. He had expressed a wish to be buried 'in the great aisle on the south side under the pillar next to the monument of Primate Narcissus Marsh, three days after my decease, as privately as possible, and at twelve o'clock at midnight.'

There's a memorial to Samuel Lover in the **north aisle**. Swift's Corner is in the **north transept**, and contains letters and some of his works along with the scroll he received when made a Freeman of Dublin in 1730. His table, chair and pulpit are there too. There's a memorial to Swift's servant, with an inscription that reads '*Here lieth the Body of Alexdr Mcgee servant to Dr Swift Dean of St Patricks. His Gratefull Master caused this Monument to be erected in memory of his Discretion, Fidelity and Diligence in that humble station.*' The **south aisle** has a memorial to Douglas Hyde, the first President of Ireland (see page 65), whose funeral took place here, causing much angst for his mainly Catholic government officials and dignitaries. In those days it was forbidden for a Catholic to attend a service in a non-Catholic establishment.

Beside Hyde's memorial there's one to poet Sir Samuel Ferguson who was President of the Royal Irish Academy.

Leave the cathedral by the main door and turn left, passing by the small **graveyard** where playwrights Lennox Robinson and Denis Johnston have adjoining graves. You are now in **St Patrick's Close**. A little bit further on to the left is **Marsh's Library (2)**. This was built by Narcissus Marsh, Archbishop of Dublin and a former Provost of Trinity College, to accommodate his library. It was the first public library in Ireland and books were so precious that readers were locked into special wire cages to stop them making off with them. It didn't stop Swift making notes on them though! When not reading in the library, William Carleton, Charles Maturin, and James Joyce also wrote there, and Maturin's son, William, later became one of the librarians. The library may be visited.

Take a left onto Kevin Street Upper and the next left into Bride Street until you come to the beautiful city oasis that is **St Patrick's Park (3)**. This was restored for the Dublin Millennium in 1988, thanks to the generosity of Jameson Irish Whiskey and the publicans of Dublin.

If you go inside you'll find the **Literary Parade**, a series of brass plaques set into the arched alcoves of the redbrick east wall of the park. These have the sculpted heads and a listing of the notable works of writers Beckett, Behan, Joyce, Mangan, O'Casey, Shaw, Swift, Synge, Wilde,Yeats, Eilís Dillon and Austin Clarke. The beginning of the parade is marked with a bigger plaque bearing the inscription:

'One of Dublin's major contrib - utions to European civilisation has been in the area of literature. It is remarkable that so many writers of world renown were born here including three winners of the Nobel Prize for Literature. This Literary Parade honours some of our distinguished sons of literature.'

The park has a boundary with Bull Ally Street – where writer and *Spectator* co-founder Sir Richard Steele was born. It was also the site of the Cerebral Palsy Clinic, which young Christy Brown used to attend, before it moved to Sandymount.

Exit the park onto **Bride Street**. Look right, towards Golden Lane, cast your eyes upwards and you will see that the modern buildings on your right are decorated with **ceramic discs** depicting scenes from *Gulliver Travels*. Take the first right after Chancery Lane onto Little Ship Street and continue around to where it joins Great Ship Street. You will come to gates leading into Dublin Castle and on your left is another gate, with a plaque that says **Hoey's Court (4)** on the left arch. It was here that Swift was born, but the site has long since been cleared and rebuilt. *Diversion: go through the gate straight ahead and you'll find the* **Chester Beatty Library (5)** *on the right side, in the gardens of* **Dublin Castle (6)**. *Bram Stoker worked in*

Dublin Castle for a time and poet Thomas Tickell and Joseph Addison had their apartments there too.

Come back up Ship Street, take a right onto Werburgh Street, the location of Mr Courtney's Academy where poet James Clarence Mangan went as a boy. On the right side is **St Werburgh's Church (7)**, where Swift's friend Dr Patrick Delany was rector. At the crossroads you'll see the **Bull & Castle (8)** at 5 Lord Edward Street, which was where Mangan's father had his general provisions store. Cross the road and walk past the side of **Christchurch Cathedral (9)**, keeping it on your left. If you're puzzled by the fact that Dublin has two great cathedrals so close to each other the explanation is simple. Christchurch was built within the walls of the original city – and St Patrick's without, in what was known as the Liberties.

You're now in **Fishamble Street (10)**, site of the Old Musick Hall, where Mr and Mrs Owenson, parents of Sydney, later Lady Morgan, would eventually live. It was here at the new Music Hall that composer George Frideric Handel premiered his oratorio *Messiah* with boys from the combined choirs of Christchurch and St Patrick's Cathedrals. Every year on the anniversary, 13 April, there is an outdoor performance on Fishamble Street where the public are invited to join in.

Halfway down, take a right into Essex Street West, which used to be known as Smock Alley, home of the theatre of the same name. The first Theatre Royal was opened in 1662 in **Smock Alley (11)**, where Richard Brinsley Sheridan's father was actor and manager. The Gaiety School of Acting is currently managing a **110-seat black box space** on the theatre's former site and work is underway to reinstate Smock Alley Theatre to its former glory.

*Diversion: **12 Parliament Street (12)**, on your right, was the hub of the Irish People newspaper. Charles Stewart Parnell's sister, Fanny, was a contributor, and other names associated with the publication were novelist and poet Charles Kickham, Thomas Caulfield Irwin and John O'Leary.*

Essex Street West becomes Essex Street East, continue along, past **The New Theatre (13)** building on your right and the **Temple Bar Culture Box (14)** on the left at number 12, turn right into Temple Lane South, then left into Cecilia Street. At number 3, **Cecilia House (15)** is built on the site of the famous **Crow Street Theatre**. It was built in 1836 by the Company of Apothecaries and was later taken over by the Medical School of the Catholic University of Ireland. Both Oliver St John Gogarty and James Joyce were students of the school, to which Edward Martyn donated his body for medical science. Turn right on to Crow Street; at the top of this you'll reach Dame Street.

*Diversion: If you turn right and walk up a little way you'll see the canopy over the modest entrance to the **Olympia Theatre (16)**. Dating back to the 1800s, this Victorian music hall-style theatre presents an eclectic schedule of variety shows, musicals, operettas, concerts, ballet, comedy and drama. The Victorian canopy was replaced in the 1980s but in 2004 was demolished when clipped by an articulated truck. It has since been restored using photographs of the original.*

Turn left onto Dame Street, cross over and take a right into Trinity Street, turn left into Andrew's Street, where on your right you'll see the former **church of St Andrew (17)**. This is where Swift's other love, Esther Van Homrigh (Vanessa) is buried, as are her sister and father. It's no longer used as a church but as the main office for **Dublin Tourism**. It's also where you can buy tickets for the Dublin Literary Pub Crawl. Go left along Andrew's Street onto College Green where you have to cross over Dame Street to **Foster Place (18)**, which

was once a row of very fashionable houses and where the Van Homrighs resided. It was then known as Turnstile Alley. It's now home to the **Wax Museum at number 4**. Continue around the **Bank of Ireland (19)**, which used to be our Houses of Parliament, and you'll come to the junction with Fleet Street. Here, on your left, you'll find the **Palace Bar (20)**, beloved of certain gentlemen of the fourth estate. James Joyce, Brendan Behan, Patrick Kavanagh and Flann O'Brien were just four of its famous regulars. The Pearl Bar was another favourite haunt, especially when *The Irish Times* was located on the same street. The Pearl Bar is no more, but tales of lunch times and evenings spent there still abound among men and women of the press corps whenever they get together. Cross Westmoreland Street into the continuation of Fleet Street on your right, take a left into **D'Olier Street** where Samuel Lover used to live at **number 9 (21)**.

Take a right at the end of D'Olier Street onto Burgh Quay, then right into **Hawkin's Street (22)** where Samuel Lover exhibited paintings at the Royal Dublin Society, then based there. This street was once the location of the Theatre Royals. Yes, there were three different ones on this site, the first opened in 1821 and the last closed in 1862. It was here that Dion Boucicault returned from the US to put his *Arrah-na-Pogue* on stage.

A left turn will take you into Poolbeg Street and to **Mulligan's Pub (23)**, affectionately known as 'the sub office' by staff of the now defunct *Irish Press*. It's unpretentious, full of dark mahogany, atmosphere and walls decorated with posters from the Theatre Royal. Mulligans features in *Counterparts* in James Joyce's *Dubliners*, when a group ends up there on a drunken meander when the Scotch House was closed.

Go to the end and turn right onto Tara Street and right at the end onto Pearse Street. Cross over to **Trinity College (24)** and proceed right, along by the college railings. This will take you to the front gates with their tantalising glimpse of the cobbled quadrangle beyond, where Oscar Wilde and his brother Willie, as well as Charles Lever all had rooms. You'll sense the echoes of the footsteps of Swift and Berkeley, Congreve and Farquhar, Synge and Beckett as you savour the ambience. Make sure to go in and view the world-famous **Book of Kells** in the Treasury of the Library, which now has a special exhibition on the Book, called 'Turning Darkness Into Light', then make time to visit the Long Room Library. The Douglas Hyde Theatre is also located on the campus.

Leaving the college by the main entrance, retrace your steps back into **Pearse Street**. This used to be Brunswick Street but its name was changed in honour of brothers Patrick and Willie Pearse, who were born at **number 27 (25)**, on the left, and who were executed for their part in the 1916 Rising. The building at number 27 still carries the sign, Pearse & Sons, Ecclesiastical and Architectural Sculptors, and there's a stone memorial on the house.

Further along on the left you'll see **St Mark's Church, at number 42 (26)**, where Oscar Wilde was christened Oscar Fingal O'Flahertie Wills Wilde. A few doors from it, near the junction with Lombard Street and Westland Row, **number 52 (27)** is the building that housed the Antient Concert Rooms where George Bernard Shaw's mother used to sing under the name of Hilda. That later became the Academy Cinema and still has **The Academy** over the doorway. The Rooms were used by the members of the Irish Literary Theatre, including Yeats, Lady Gregory, George Moore, Edward Martyn and others as the location for staging plays before the establishment of the Abbey Theatre.

*Diversion: If you turn right onto Westland Row you will find **The Church of St Andrew (28)**, on the left, commonly called **Westland Row Church**. It was its Angelus bells that used to prompt Edward Martyn to say the Rosary at his window in the Kildare Street Club to annoy the other members. Behind it (entrance via Sth Cumberland Street) is the **Christian Brothers School (29)**, which the Pearse brothers attended.*

Plaques to writers Eilis Dillon and JM Synge are among those in the Literary Parade in St Patrick's Park

The Walks:3

Shaw's Birthplace to Camden Street

Newman House, 86 St Stephen's Green,
the first Catholic University of Ireland,
whose students included James Joyce
and Austin Clarke.

Key to Route 3: Shaw's Birthplace to Camden Street

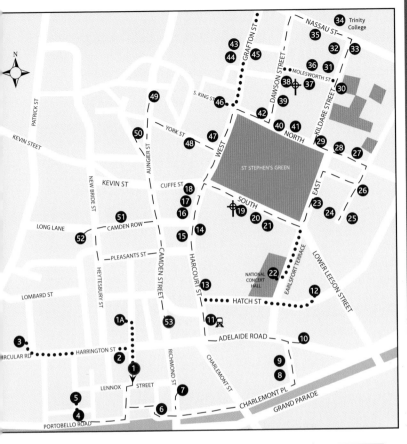

Inscription under the Setanta or Táin Wall mosaic, just off Nassau Street

Walking route 3: Shaw's Birthplace to Camden Street

Note: Buses 16, 16A, 19, 19A, 122 will bring you to Harrington Street from the city centre. The Shaw Birthplace is signposted from there.

Take the Shaw birthplace at **33 Synge Street (1)** as a starting point. (On the continuation of this street, across Harrington Street, is the famous **Synge Street Boys School (1A)** run by the Christian Brothers at **numbers 12-16**. Past pupils include Pearse Hutchinson, Todd Andrews, Brian O'Nolan, James Plunkett and Pete St John who wrote the anthem *Dublin in the Rare Auld Times*).

Number 33 is marked with a plaque, referring to Shaw as 'Author of Many Plays'. Give yourself time to visit this house where his singer mother, who used the stage name of Hilda, treated family and friends to musical evenings in the upstairs drawing room. Her teacher was Mr Vandaleur Lee and he lived at **16 Harrington Street (2)**, three houses from the corner on your left. He also kept rooms at number 11, on the right side of the junction, where he taught his music pupils.

*Diversion: AE (George Russell) lived in **33 Emorville Avenue (3)**, which you reach by taking a left on Harrington Street (which becomes South Circular Road), past number*

16, on your left, until you come to a large redbrick church, cross the road and take the next right.

Back on Synge Street, with the Shaw birthplace to your left, continue through the junction with Lennox Street, onto Lennox Place, then bear right alongside the canal on Portobello Road. James Stephens stayed at number **14 (4)**.

*Diversion: This area once had a thriving Jewish community and the **Irish Jewish Museum**, which is worth a visit, is located at **3 Walworth Road (5)**, off Portobello Road, through the junction with St Kevin's Road, and turn right.*

Turn back on Portobello Road and head along the canal towards the lock gates. The impressive building on the left of the lock, **Portobello College (6)**, was formerly Portobello Nursing Home, and before that a coaching inn. It features in Beckett's poem *Enueg* and it's where painter Jack B Yeats, brother of WB, died.

Turn left into **South Richmond Street** where Katharine Tynan lived at **25 (7)** for seven years. Head back to the canal and turn left. Proceed along by the water to the lights. Cross Charlemont Street and keep straight into Charlemont Place, where the Hilton Hotel is located; continue until you see a red brick building with a large antenna (a

Garda [Police] Station) facing you, take a left into **Harcourt Terrace. Number 5 (8)** is where AE's *Deirdre* had its first outing in 1910, in the garden of this grand house. A plaque marks the location. Forty-three years later the house next door, **number 4 (9)**, became home to the founders of the Gate Theatre, 'The Boys' Micheál MacLiammóir and Hilton Edwards. They lived here together for thirty-four years, until Micheál's death in 1978.

Continue to the junction with **Adelaide Road**, turn right and on the left side, some way down is **number 63 (10)** where Beckett went to school at the Earlsfort House School (now a modern Health Service building). Come back up Adelaide Road until you arrive at where the Luas tram lines veer right. Cross here into **Harcourt Street**. The tram stops outside the former Harcourt St **train terminus**, (now the **Odeon club/bar/restaurant**) **(11)**. This stop is referred to by Beckett in his play *That Time*. He would have used it regularly when going and coming to classes, as would students of the High School, then located across the road, before it moved to Rathgar. WB Yeats and arguably Dublin's foremost Joycean exponent, David Norris, were both pupils there.

Diversion: the next right is Hatch Street where the now demolished St Matthias Church was the setting for the marriage between Augusta Persse and Sir William Gregory in1880. Continue into Lower Hatch Street where **number 1** *is the house the Shaws shared with Mr Vandaleur Lee* **(12)**.

Back on Harcourt Street, when Shaw's mother and his sisters followed Lee to London, George and his father took lodgings at **number 60**, on your right. It's now the **Harcourt Hotel (13)**. The Standard Hotel used to be located at **79-82 (14)**, where Lady Gregory sometimes stayed. Cardinal Newman's address was **numbers 16 and 17 (15)**, on the left (marked by a plaque) where his friend had a boarding school; twenty years later, Bram Stoker also lived at 16. Diarist Jonah Barrington lived at **14 (16)** and this is where his wife used to annoy their neighbours, Lord and Lady Clonmel, by sitting in the side window overlooking their garden and keeping tabs on their comings and goings. A street across the road is now called Clonmel Street after them. Cardinal Newman eventually opted for a more permanent stay at **number 6**, now **Conradh na Gaeilge (17)**, on the left. Next door, **number 5 (18)**, bears a plaque to George Fitzmaurice, an

Abbey playwright.

You are now on the south side of St Stephen's Green. Development has seen the demolition of the elegant Russell Hotel on the right corner, where Lady Gregory was a regular visitor. It had previously been a nursing home where novelist Annie M P Smithson had done her nursing training. Continue right, and a few houses down was the site of the Wesleyan Connexional School where Shaw spent an abysmally unhappy year. Further along, past the Dept of Justice building and wedged between the houses, is the deceptively unremarkable entrance to **Newman's University Church (19)**. Go inside and revise your first impressions! Next to this are **numbers 85 and 86, Newman House (20)**, a glorious architectural specimen with amazing stuccowork inside. This was the first **Catholic University of Ireland**, which opened in1854 with just 17 students. Its hall of fame includes James Joyce, Thomas Kettle, Austin Clarke, Patrick Colum, Thomas MacDonagh, Patrick Pearse and Denis Florence MacCarthy. Gerard Manley Hopkins taught Greek there. Newman House is open to the public and houses the UCD Press in the basement.

Numbers 80 and 81 are now **Iveagh House (21)**, the headquarters of the Department of Foreign Affairs. This was originally built as two houses designed by Richard Castle in 1736 and remodelled by Benjamin Guinness in 1826. Mrs Mary Pendarves (see page 190), later Mrs Patrick Delany, stayed next door at number 80 and recorded her impressions of the décor for posterity. Continue to the end of the street.

Diversion: if you turn to your right into **Earlsfort Terrace**, *the block is almost completely taken over by a large grey building which housed University College Dublin for many years before its move to the new greenfield campus at Belfield, Stillorgan. It's now home to the* **National Concert Hall (22)**. *Opposite this was the former site of Alexandra College Girls School, which John Kells Ingram helped to set up and where poet Máire Mhac an tSaoi was a teacher.*

Back on the main route, cross the road and go straight ahead, keeping the Green on your left. **Loreto College**, at **number 53 (23)**, on the right, is where Mary Lavin was a pupil and then a teacher of French. Take the next right into Hume Street and continue to the junction with Ely Place; turn right into **Ely Place Upper**. This was a proper little literary colony and was once closed off with a gated entrance. The houses are numbered separately to

Ely Place proper. Sadly, many of the houses of note have been demolished in the name of progress. Go to the end of the cul de sac. Oliver St John Gogarty, surgeon and writer, lived at **15** and had his consulting rooms at street level. The building that replaced his is now the **RHA Gallery (24)**. Opposite, AE lived at **number 3 (25)** when he was involved in the Dublin Theosophical Society. He then recommended **number 4** to George Moore, who turned out to be a not-so-nice neighbour, lowering the tone of the area by painting his hall door a garish colour! When word of the neighbours' discontent reached him he decided to retaliate. He would run his cane along the railings, annoying their dogs and working them up to a barking frenzy. The neighbours got even by hiring an organ grinder to play his tinny tunes outside number 4 when Moore was writing. Walk back from the cul de sac up Ely Place. At **number 8 Ely House (26)**, on your right, another eminent surgeon, Sir Thornly Stoker, brother of Bram Stoker, resided. This house has a wonderfully decorative interior and is currently the headquarters for the **Knights of St Columbanus**. It was used as the British Embassy in the BBC drama *The Ambassador*. **Number 1** on the corner belonged to Constance Lloyd's aunt and it was here that Constance accepted Oscar Wilde's proposal of marriage. At some stage the hall door moved around to open on **Lower Baggot Street**, so the address is now **149 (27)**.

Turn left here into Merrion Row and back on to St Stephen's Green. Immediately before the Shelbourne Hotel, at **number 33 (28)** there's a **wall plaque** showing where Oliver St John Gogarty had his consulting rooms for a few years.

The Shelbourne Hotel (29) is the Grande Dame of Dublin. It's evocatively painted in Elizabeth Bowen's book, *The Shelbourne*. The Horseshoe Bar has been the venue for many discussions as to the placement of an apostrophe, the phrasing of a poem, and the clauses in literary contracts. George Moore wintered here in 1883/83 when he wrote a goodly portion of *A Drama in Muslin*. And Oscar Wilde was staying here when he went across to Ely Place to propose. Many visiting authors are interviewed in the Lord Mayor's Lounge, so stopping in here for a coffee may afford a glimpse of a famous one. James Stephens took refuge in the hotel during the Easter Rising and wrote an eyewitness account of the happenings in *The Insurrection of*

Dublin. He described seeing the women of Baggot Street outside the hotel serving tea and bread to the soldiers.

Take the first right into **Kildare Street**. Christy Brown married Mary Carr in the Central Registry Office, which was located on the left before you come to the Department of Enterprise building. It has since relocated from this street. On your right are the **National Museum**, **Leinster House**, home of the Dáil (the Irish Parliament), and the **National Library (30)**. Oliver St John Gogarty met Joyce for the first time by accident in the National Library, where Lady Gregory used to go to work on her translations. The Library also features in *Ulysses*. The Metropolitan School of Art, where AE and Jack Yeats were students, used to be behind the National Library. It too has moved and changed its name to the National College of Art and Design. Bram Stoker had a flat in number 30, **now 35 (31)** on the left, but the plaque that used to mark the house has disappeared! Lady Morgan (Sydney Owenson) lived in number 35 for eighteen years. It was later renumbered **39 (32)** and is marked by a plaque. At the end of the street, at **number 1 (33)** on the right, is the former premises of the Kildare Street Club, founded in 1782,

where Edward Martyn fell foul of his peers. It's now the headquarters of the ***Alliance Française*** in Dublin. The club later moved to St Stephen's Green, to a stately early Georgian residence built in 1776 for Joseph Leeson, after whom several roads are called in Dublin 2. It amalgamated with the University Club and is still in existence.

You are now facing the boundary wall of **Trinity College (34)**. Behind that is the cricket green where Oscar Wilde and Samuel Beckett played. Turn left onto **Nassau Street**. Nora Barnacle and James Joyce met on this street and novelist Annie M P Smithson lived here, just one of her many addresses. You'll pass the junction with **Frederick Street** on the left where the Nassau Hotel used to be, from **numbers 16-20 (35)**. Correspondence exists from July 1900 between Maud Gonne when she was a guest in the Nassau and William Butler Yeats, then in Paris. Yeats also stayed there occasionally and diarist Jonah Barrington lodged on this street too.

Continue along Nassau Street and take a left onto **Dawson Street**, with its bookshops so beloved of contemporary writer John Boyne. On the first corner there used to be a hotel called Morrisons and its guest book contained the names of Charles Stewart Parnell, Yeats and

Charles Dickens. Dickens wrote from there to Mrs Rutherford on 25 August 1858, graciously declining an invitation due to his commitments in Dublin, declaring 'I am virtually a galley slave.'

Diversion: Halfway up Dawson Street take a left into **Molesworth Street**. *It was here, at* **number 15 (36)**, *(the black door on your left) that the land agents Charles Uniacke and Thomas Townshend were based and where George Bernard Shaw had his first job, progressing to chief cashier. Charles Lever had lodgings at* **number 33 (37)** *on the right. The Leinster Hall used to be on this street, where the first President of Ireland, Douglas Hyde, delivered an address on 'the necessity of de-Anglicising the Irish people.' Return to the junction with Dawson Street and turn left.*

Sir Joshua Dawson and Viscount Molesworth were responsible for building many of Dublin's streets around here. Dawson Street dates back to 1709 and Molesworth Street to 1925. Sir Joshua donated the land for **St Anne's Church (38)** on the left, which was completed in 1725. This has several literary connections. One of its rectors was Daniel Hearn, Lafcadio Hearn's great-great-grandfather. Poet and parishioner Felicia Hemans is buried here; she has a stained glass window dedicated to her memory. Percy French once lived on the street and Dracula's creator Bram Stoker married his Florence there – she had previously been expected to marry Oscar Wilde, but he did write to wish her luck on her marriage.

Carry on past the **Mansion House (39)** on the left, home of Dublin's Lord Mayor. At the top of the street you will find yourself back on St Stephen's Green. Should you go left you'd pass the former site of St Andrew's School at **number 21 (40)**. It was the alma mater of playwright Denis Johnston. Also on the left is the **Kildare Street and University Club at number 17 (41)**.

Take a right in the direction of Grafton Street and this will take you past the **Stephen's Green Hibernian Club** at **number 9 (42)**, which Cardinal Newman had considered joining so that he'd have somewhere decent to go for his food. He never did.

Diversion: At the end of the street, **Grafton Street** *beckons to the right. This is Dublin's main shopping street where Elizabeth Bowen recalled the gentry keeping appointments with their milliners while they prepared for 'the season'.*

Samuel Lover was born at

number 60 (43), on the left, while Whyte's Academy was located at number 79. **Bewley's Café (44)** *now occupies the spot and a plaque marks the fact. Its roll call included Thomas Moore, Robert Emmet, Isaac Weld and Richard Brinsley Sheridan. There was a famous bookshop called Mr Milliken's on Grafton Street, which was frequented by Trinity students and other interested parties, including Percy Bysshe Shelley and his wife who lived nearby in* **number 17 (45)**. *Rudyard Kipling and his wife stopped in too. The* Dublin Penny Journal, *dated December 15, 1832 records that Sir Walter Scott spent 'upwards of £60 in the purchase of books relating solely to the history and antiquities of this country.'*

If you intend to finish your walk you'd be well advised to stay away from the popular pubs with literary ties around these parts and come back again later. (see section on Literary Pubs, page 169). The best loved around here are McDaid's in Harry Street, the Bailey and The Duke in Duke Street, the first stop on the Dublin Literary Pub Crawl. Walk back up the street until you are facing the Stephen's Green Shopping Centre.

As you cross the junction with **South King Street**, look to your right and you will see the **Gaiety Theatre** **(46)**. Many well-known actors and performers have had their handprints immortalised in the pavement outside the Theatre.

Continue along the Green until you come to the headquarters of the **Royal College of Surgeons in Ireland** at **number 123 (47)** on your right. Sir William Wilde, father of Oscar, is mentioned among its notable alumni. Turn right after this into **York Street (48)**. This was home to several writers, but the buildings fell into disrepair, many becoming tenements, and were eventually knocked down, so there is nothing remaining of the residences. Like that of poet James Clarence Mangan, who was observed at number 6, looking very poorly (he was noted for his pallor) by writer Annie MP Smithson, who covered this district as a nurse. Number 44 was home to Charles Maturin, who was visited there by Robert Carelton. People used to stop and watch through the curtains to see Maturin dancing, something he seemed to do quite a lot.

Continue straight through the crossroads with Mercer Street and at the next intersection you'll be in **Aungier Street**. Take a right and you'll come to **number 12 (49)** where poet and bard Thomas Moore was born and raised. Come back up Aungier Street. On the right is the

YMCA building (50), the original site of Maturin's parish church, and the graveyard where he was buried was one of several Huguenot burial places in Dublin. The churchyard was in use until 1883. The church was demolished in the 1980s and all the remains were re-interred in Mount Jerome Cemetery.

Continue along Aungier Street, which becomes **Wexford Street** and then **Camden Street**. At **Whelan's pub** on your right, take a right onto **Camden Row**. **St Kevin's Churchyard (51)**, now a public park, is tucked away on the right. Thomas Moore's parents and sister Ellen are buried here. The inscription on Ellen's headstone concludes with the words 'deeply mourned by her brother Thomas Moore, the bard of his much loved country Ireland.'

Continue to the end of Camden Row. Facing you is the former **Meath Hospital (52)**. Brendan Behan and James Clarence Mangan died here and Oliver St John Gogarty was one of its esteemed consultants.

Turn left and continue to the next corner and left again into **Pleasant's Street**. Go to the end and turn right and you're back in **Camden Street**. Turn right here and cross the road and where it forks you'll find the famous **Bleeding Horse Pub (53)**, one of Dublin's oldest and most historic establishments. Dating from 1649, it has been frequented over the years by literary greats such as Joyce, Le Fanu, Mangan, Gogarty and Donleavy and immortalised in some of their writings.

The Gaiety Theatre

The house where Oscar Wilde grew up, 1 Merrion Square

The Walks 4 :

The National Gallery to Lower Baggot St

Key to Route 4: The National Gallery to Lower Baggot St

1 The National Gallery of Ireland
2 Site of Greene's Bookshop
3 1 /2 Leinster Street
4 32 Lincoln Place
5 Kennedy's Pub
6 Sweny's, Druggist & Chemist
7 36 Westland Row
8 21 Westland Row
9 Westland Row Church
10 CBS, Sth Cumberland Street
11 The Ginger Man Pub
12 Wilde house/1 Merrion Square
13 Oscar Wilde Statue
14 84 Merrion Square South
15 82 Merrion Square South
16 70 Merrion Square South
17 42 Merrion Square East
18 National Maternity Hospital
19 19 Mount Street Lower
20 11 Warrington Place
21 15 Warrington Place
22 25 Herbert Place
23 15 Herbert Place
24 35 Haddington Road
25 National Print Museum
26 Baggot Street Hospital
27 The Waterloo
28 Searsons Pub
29 38 Baggot Street Upper
30 62 Pembroke Road
31 Raglan Road
32 St Bartholomew's, Clyde Road

33 54 Wellington Road
34 18 Waterloo Road
35 73 Upper Leeson Street
36 119 Upper Leeson Street
37 136 Upper Leeson Street
38 Christ Church
39 4 Upper Leeson Street
40 35 Mespil Road
41 Kavanagh/Percy French Seats
42 Kavanagh Statue, Wilton Tce
43 Court Apartments
44 1 Wilton Place
45 67 Lower Baggot Street
46 15 Lower Baggot Street
47 15 Herbert Street
48 Pepper Canister Church (St Stephen's)
49 37 Upper Mount Street
50 38 Upper Mount Street
51 50 Upper Mount Street
52 29 Fitzwilliam Street Lower
53 United Arts Club, 3 Upper Fitzwilliam Street
54 18 Fitzwilliam Square South
55 42 Fitzwilliam Square West
56 60 Fitzwilliam Square North
57 13 Fitzwilliam Place
58 42 Fitzwilliam Place
59 133 Lower Baggot Street
60 Toners, 139 Lower Baggot Street

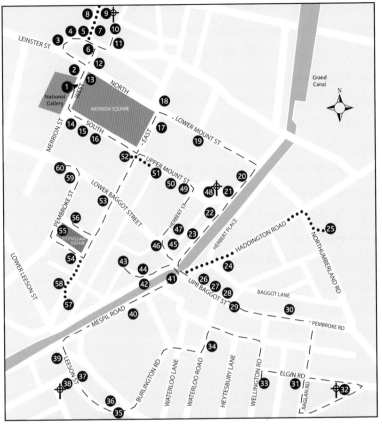

Walking route 4: The National Gallery to Lower Baggot Stree

Using the **National Gallery of Ireland (1)** on Merrion Square West as a starting point, it seems appropriate to pop inside and have a look at both the Shaw Room and the statue of George Bernard Shaw in the Atrium. The Gallery has benefited hugely from the bequest by Shaw of a third of the proceeds from his published works, and particularly from the success of his *Pygmalion* (filmed and produced on stages around the world as *My Fair Lady*). While you are there you might also take time to view the gallery's portrait collection which includes paintings of many of the writers whom you will have met in the pages of this book, including WB Yeats, Lady Gregory, Shaw, Thomas Moore, AE, Douglas Hyde, Jonathan Swift, Maeve Binchy.

Leave the gallery by the **Clare Street** entrance and you'll exit onto the street where diarist Jonah Barrington used to live while at Trinity College. This street also housed one of Dublin's best-loved bookshops, **Greene's (2)**, at **number 16**, with its bookstalls outside and booksellers who knew every title in their vast library of antiquarian and first edition books. Sadly, this is no more, although you can still see the curved wrought-iron hanger for the Greene's sign over the tailoring shop that has replaced it. Greene's itself now operates as an on-line shop in Sandyford, County Dublin. It features in Beckett's *Dream of Fair to Middling Women*, perhaps because he used to enjoy perusing the shelves and observing the comings and goings from his room in the top floor of number 6 across the street.

Clare Street joins Leinster Street South here at the end of the Trinity railings. **Numbers 1 and 2 Leinster Street (3)** was the site of Finn's Hotel, the place of employment of chambermaid Nora Barnacle, whom Joyce was later to marry.

Take the left fork past the **Lincoln's Inn pub** on your left, into **Lincoln Place**, which skirts round the end of Trinity College Park. Edward Martyn roomed along here at one stage. St Mark's Ophthalmic and Aural Hospital was located behind Trinity College at **32 Lincoln Place (4)**. This was Sir William Wilde's hospital and it was there he treated a young Sean O'Casey for the eye complaint that prevented him going to school for a period. It later amalgamated with the Royal Victoria Eye and Ear Hospital on Adelaide Road.

A little further along you'll find yourself outside **Kennedy's pub (5)** on the left, which is referred to by Beckett. Before it was a public house this was a general grocery where young Oscar Wilde worked at one stage, stacking the shelves. On the other side of the road, just before the corner, is **Sweny's, Druggist and Chemist (6)**, where Joyce's Leopold Bloom waited amid the smell of sponges and loofas to buy his four-penny cake of sweet lemony soap. It closed as a pharmacy in 2009, but is still very much alive and open and run by enthusiastic volunteers who hold readings and storytelling amid books and old photos and sweet, waxy, lemony soap. www.sweny.ie

*Diversion: Turn left into **Westland Row. Number 36 (7)** is where Synge attended music lessons at the Royal Academy of Music. Maura Laverty based her* Lift up Your Gates *novel around the slums in this neighbourhood; it was later adapted as* Tolka Row, *RTÉ's first soap opera. On the left, at **number 21 (8)**, was the home of Sir William Wilde and his wife Speranza. This was where Oscar was born. It is now the **Oscar Wilde Centre for Irish Writing**, School of English, Trinity College. The plaque on the building states* Poet, Dramatist Wit Oscar Wilde do rugadh sa teach seo *16.10. 1854 (... was born in this house 16.10.54).*

Westland Row Church (9) is on the other side of the street, beside **Pearse Street Railway Station**, so called because the Pearse brothers, Patrick and Willie, lived and went to the **Christian Brothers School** (entrance on Sth Cumberland Street) **(10)** close by. The church is the one where Brendan Behan and Beatrice Salkeld got married in 1955.

Back on the main walk continue straight on to **Fenian Street**. If you look left you'll see the **Ginger Man** pub, at **number 40 (11)**, which, although not there in the time of Donleavy's Trinity days, is a good representation of an authentic pub with well-thumbed book and literary memorabilia all over the place.

Double back around the **Davenport Hotel** and walk up to the junction with Merrion Square North. The house on the corner, **number 1 Merrion Square (12)**, is now the **American College in Dublin**, but its claim to fame is that it's where Oscar Wilde grew up and where his parents held their salons. There are two plaques on the front of the building, one for Oscar and one for his father, Sir William Wilde. The house also has a stained glass window, which can be seen from Merrion Street Lower, depicting a scene from *The Happy Prince*, one of Oscar's stories for children. This is by Irish artist Peadar Lamb and was unveiled by Oscar's grandson, Merlin Holland. And, a little gem of trivia: this is where Joyce arranged to meet Nora Barnacle for the first time and she stood him up!

Directly opposite the house, just inside **Merrion Square** (officially called Archbishop Ryan Park) railings, there's a **statue of Oscar Wilde (13)**, best viewed from either side rather than straight on as its two profiles sum up the man - sardonic and pensive. It's a beautiful piece of work with terrific detail, capturing this flamboyant character in his iconic smoking jacket in jade, with pink thulite for the padded collar and cuffs. His shoes are polished black marble. It was commissioned by the Guinness Group, created by Danny Osborne and erected in 1977. The head had to be replaced in 2010 as a few cracks had appeared. The replacement was done by the original artist, who crafted it out of white jadeite jade.

Merrion Square became a very fashionable Georgian Square, with numerous professional people living and having consulting rooms there, and the number of heritage plaques fixed to the walls around the Square attest to that. However it was not always so and quite close by very

large families lived in overcrowded conditions with no sanitary facilities at all. 'The residents of Merrion Square may be surprised to hear,' wrote Dr Whitely Stokes in 1799, 'that in the angle behind Mount Street and Holles Street there is now a family of ten in a very small room, of whom eight have had fever in the last month'. Whitley's great-great-grandson, who bore the same name, was born in number 5. He was a Celtic scholar of note.

Cross the road, and with the Wilde statue on your left, walk up **Merrion Square West**, passing the National Gallery on your right. Take the next left into **Merrion Square South**. On this side the heritage plaques include ones for **AE** who lived at **number 84 (14), WB Yeats at number 82 (15)** and **Joseph Sheridan le Fanu at number 70 (16)**. Take a left around the park onto **Merrion Square East** where Jonah Barrington lived at **42 (17)**. At the end of the road, across the street, is the **National Maternity Hospital (18)**, where Brendan Behan was born. Its entrance is on Holles Street. This Dublin hospital features in *Ulysses*.

Take a right onto **Mount Street Lower**, which was where Thomas Davis began his education at Mr Mangan's School. JM Synge died at **number 19 (19)**, then the Elphis Nursing Home. He had written from there saying he had had 'a rather severe' operation, but that he 'was able to see people now if WB.Y [Yeats] should be in town again.' Beckett makes reference to this establishment in his short story collection *More Pricks than Kicks*.

If you continue down this street you'll reach the **Grand Canal** where you should turn right into **Warrington Place**. Thomas Davis's family lived here before moving to Baggot Street. John O'Leary lived at **number 11 (20)** and Le Fanu had two addresses on this stretch, including **15 Warrington Place (21)**.

If you continue along here, with the canal on your left, you'll enter **Herbert Place**, where Brian O'Nolan's family moved into **number 25 (22)**. Elizabeth Bowen was born and spent her formative years in **number 15 (23)**, later prompting her to write *Seven Years, Memories of a Dublin Childhood*. In this she describes going to her dancing lesson, shopping in Baggot Street and walking around this neighbourhood. Patrick Kavanagh and his brother, Peter, shared accommodation at numerous addresses in the vicinity. Both were regulars in Parson's Bookshop, which used to be just after the bridge on the right. Important patrons were encouraged to sign their name in the visitors' book.

Brendan Behan was a regular there too. Turn left, cross the bridge.

Diversion: Turn left again to **Haddington Road**, *where Patrick Kavanagh lived in a flat at* **35 (24)**. *It's worth continuing almost to the end of this road, because behind the grey stone wall of Beggar's Bush you'll find the* **National Print Museum (25)** *in the courtyard, complete with wonderful memorabilia from the pre-computer era of hot metal. Allow time to explore this! Come back to main route.*

Back on the main route, carry straight on to **Baggot Street Upper**. In the next block is the imposing façade of the former **Baggot Street Hospital (26)**, then you'll pass two well-loved pubs, the **Waterloo (27)** and **Searson's (28)**, compulsory refreshment stops for the likes of Kavanagh and his associates. Denis Florence McCarthy, who was the first professor of English Literature at the Catholic University, after abandoning his studies for the priesthood, lived at **38 (29)** beside the Waterloo. He went on to father nine children.

Continue into **Pembroke Road**. On your left is **number 62(30)**, the place where Kavanagh resided for the longest time; a plaque marks the spot. Cross over and take the next right into **Raglan Road (31)**, immortalised forever in Kavanagh's poem of the same name, set to music and recorded by numerous artists, including Luke Kelly and Sinead O'Connor. Short story master Frank O'Connor lived in a flat on this road while he was working at Pembroke Library on Anglesea Road, Ballsbridge.

Go to the end of Raglan Road, turn left onto **Clyde Road**, and you'll come upon the beautiful church of **St Bartholomew's (32)**, on your left, which the Bowen family used to attend occasionally. Take a left onto **Elgin Road**, then at the third junction take a left into **Wellington Road**. A little way down is **number 54 (33)** where Denis Johnston lived. When Lady Gregory rejected one of his plays for the Abbey, he changed the name and sent it to the Gate, who produced it.

Come back to the crossing, then take the next left into Pembroke Lane to the junction with **Waterloo Road**. Turn left. Along here at **number 18 (34)** on the left is the house where Brendan Behan and his new bride Beatrice Salkeld had their first home, in the ground floor flat.

Take the turn opposite you into **Burlington Road**. Continue to the end of the road.

Cross the junction and take the lefthand fork, back towards the city centre, along **Upper Leeson Street**.

Lafcadio Hearn lived at **number 73 (35)** as a child. Hearn is still a much-respected writer in Japan and is honoured with a statue in Matsue. He's also mentioned by James Bond in *You Only Live Twice*.

Thomas Kettle lived at **number 119 (36)** on this street. And yes, you've guessed it; Kavanagh lived along here too, at **number 136 (37)** on the right.

The grandiose church complex on the left was where George Bernard Shaw went to Sunday school – and hated it. It was then the Methodist Molyneux Church. It was subsequently renamed **Christ Church (38)**; this closed for services in 2005 and is now used by the Romanian Orthodox Church in Dublin. A little further along in the next terrace Mr Harrick's Classical and English School, one of the schools attended by Synge, was located at **number 4 (39)**.

Before Leeson Street Bridge turn right into Sussex Terrace and straight into **Mespil Road**, a favourite walk of many. If you look right you'll see the **Mespil flats** complex, where Frank O'Connor lived for a time. Percy French lived at **number 35 Mespil Road (40)**. On the canal bank near the lock gates are two seats **(41)** commemorating Percy French and Patrick Kavanagh. On Percy French's seat is inscribed:

'Remember me is all I ask, and yet

If remembrance prove a task forget'

Kavanagh's seat (not to be confused with the statue of Kavanagh on a bench on the other side of the canal) has his birth and death dates inscribed on the granite sides and was erected by some of his friends who knew how much he loved this spot. It was unveiled on St Patrick's Day 1968 and each year on that day followers gather to remember him and read his *Lines Written on a Seat on the Grand Canal in Dublin*.

Cross the canal on the footbridge at the lock onto **Wilton Terrace**, where you'll find a marvellous **statue of Kavanagh (42)**, reclining on a bench, executed by sculptor John Coll, and erected as part of Dublin City of Culture in1991. The shoelaces are untied, something that Kavanagh was noted for!

A short distance from here are the **Court Apartments (43)** in Wilton Place where Liam O'Faherty, one of the founder members of the Irish Academy of Letters and Frank O'Connor, master of the short story, had flats. Kavanagh also lived in Wilton Place for a time, at **number 1 (44)**.

From Baggot Street Bridge turn left into **Lower Baggot Street** and cross over. Here you'll find **number 67(45)**, home of Thomas Davis's mother, where he died, aged 30, of tuberculosis or scarlet fever, both incurable diseases in the 1800s. He was a nationalist, poet, writer and co-founder of the weekly newspaper, *The Nation*. Brendan Behan had rooms in **number 15 (46)** for a while.

Turn right into **Herbert Street**, where Behan also lived at **number 15 (47)**. Beckett's mother, May Barclay, died in the Merrion Nursing Home which used to be here. A short way further along you'll meet **Upper Mount Street**, but it's worth diverting a little here. On your right at the end of the street is an imposing church which forms its own traffic island and is referred to by Dubliners as the **Pepper Canister Church (48)**. Its official title is St Stephen's. It's where Percy French married his first wife, Ettie, and the church where the funeral service for Yeats's brother was held. It is believed to have been where the Bowen family habitually worshipped when in their summer home at 15 Herbert Place.

Parallel to Herbert Street, tucked away in what would have been the alleyway leading to the coach houses, there used to be a very small theatre called **The Pike**. Little did those meagre audiences who attended fledgling works realise that they were witnessing the beginning of greatness – both from Behan, who premiered *The Quare Fella* there in 1955, or from Beckett, whose *Waiting for Godot* received a mixed reaction the following year.

Turn left into **Upper Mount Street** where Kavanagh lodged in **number 37 (49)**. The house next door, **number 38 (50)**, was the John Kells Ingram home and John Betjeman had his offices at **number 50 (51)** when he was press attaché in Ireland for the British Government.

Diversion: At the end of Upper Mount Street on your left is Fitzwilliam Street Lower. Number 29 (52), on the corner with Merrion Square Sth is a fully restored Georgian house which is open to the public as a museum. This gives you a real insight into what life was like when this elegant square was built. The house was restored for Dublin's Millennium in 1988 by the Electricity Supply Board, who had pulled down sixteen Georgian houses in Lower Fitzwilliam Street some years earlier to create their modern offices, causing uproar among conservationists.

Turn left into **Fitzwilliam Street** and continue into **Upper Fitzwilliam Street**. On the far side, **number 3 (53)** is where the United Arts Club has its home since its foundation in 1907. This was formed with a view to *'combining the unusual advantages of a social club, open to both ladies and gentlemen, with features of special interest to workers in Art, in Music, and in Literature.'*

Irish PEN holds its monthly meetings there. Amongst its past members were Percy French and WB Yeats. If you continue along you will come to Fitzwilliam Square, where WB's brother, painter Jack B Yeats, lived and worked at **number 18 Fitzwilliam Square South (54)**. Before moving out of town to Rathfarnham, WB lived at **number 42** on the **west side** of the Square (55) and Denis Johnston on the **north side** in **number 60 (56)**.

*Diversion: Continue past Fitzwilliam Square to **Fitzwilliam Place**. Fans of Anthony Cronin will recognise the name The Catacombs, which he mentioned in two of his novels,* The Life of Riley *and* Dead as Doornails. *This used to be below stairs at number **13 Fitzwilliam Place (57)**, an informal and notorious club, which developed in the basement flat rented by one Dickie Wyman in the 1940s. He made his money by returning the empty beer bottles the next morning. Aspiring writers such as Brendan Behan, Patrick Kavanagh, and Anthony Cronin were all regulars of this after-*

hours boozing den. So too was JP Donleavy who mentions the hideaway in The Ginger Man. *James Stephens, the writer that Joyce had proposed would finish* Finnegan's Wake *for him, had a flat on the opposite side of the road at* **number 42(58)**. *He didn't have to complete that task, however, Joyce managed to do it himself.*

Back on the main route, turn left onto Fitzwilliam Square South and right again onto **Pembroke Street**. Turn left again into **Lower Baggot Street**. **Number 133 (59)** on the corner is where the Cuala Press operated. This was set up in 1908 by the Yeats sisters and played an important role in the Celtic Revival.

A little further on, at **number 139**, is **Toners** pub **(60)** where Gogarty famously tried to introduce WB Yeats to pub culture, and failed miserably – on only one sherry!

To get back to where you started your tour, continue to the next intersection and turn right –The National Gallery of Ireland is at the end on the left.

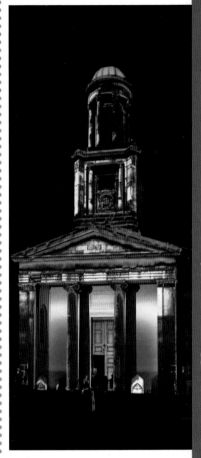

The Pepper Canister church

POET
PAINTER
ECONOMIST MYSTIC
GEORGE RUSSELL
LIVED IN THIS HOUSE
1911 - 1933
Æ

The house where George Russell (AE) lived for many years, 17 Rathgar Avenue

George Moore lived in this house at 4 Ely Place

The bust of James Clarence Mangan in
St Stephen's Green

The Writers .....

Past and Present

M-Z

Ferdia MacAnna
1955-

Born in Dublin and educated at Trinity College Dublin, Ferdia MacAnna was known to audiences as Rocky de Valera, lead singer with the Gravediggers, before finding new audiences as a writer and playwright. He has written several books, including two memoirs, *Bald Head*, *A Cancer Story* and *The Last of the Bald Heads*. His novels include *The Last of the High Kings*, which was made into a movie starring Gabriel Byrne, *Ship Inspector* and *Cartoon City*. *Mom*, his stage play, was produced in the Project Arts Centre in 1994.

Máire Mhac an tSaoi
1922–

Máire Mhac an tSaoi (Máire MacEntee) came from a distinguished pedigree, politically and academically. Her father was a former Tánaiste (deputy Prime Minister), her mother a teacher at Alexandra College. She also attended Beaufort High School in Rathfarnham and UCD. She spent much of her life in Dunquin, Dingle, County Kerry, where she became an expert in Munster Irish, her language of choice.

Her first collection, *Margadh na Saoire*, received great acclaim, as did her last one *Shoa agus Dánta Eile*. She worked for four years on Tomás de Bhaldraithe's *English-Irish Dictionary*. She also published a memoir, *The Same Age as the State* under her married name of Máire Cruise O'Brien. She was married to Conor Cruise O'Brien. (*see p37*)

Colum McCann
1965-

Dubliner Colum McCann has achieved international success through his fiction, most recently with his novel *Let the Great World Spin*, which received the 2009 National Book Award for fiction. It has been described by *Esquire* as the 'first great 9/11 novel'.

Colum has written two collections of short stories and five novels, including *This Side of Brightness*, *Dancer*, *Zoli*, *Songdogs* and *Let the Great World Spin*, all of which are international bestsellers. His fiction has been published in thirty languages and has appeared in the *New Yorker*, the *Atlantic Monthly*, *GQ*, *Paris Review*, and elsewhere. In 2003 Colum was named *Esquire* magazine's Writer of the Year. Other awards and honours include a Pushcart Prize, the Rooney Prize, the Hennessy Award for Irish Literature, the Irish Independent Hughes and Hughes/Sunday Independent Novel of the Year 2003, the 2002 Ireland Fund of Monaco Princess Grace Memorial Literary Award, and the 2009 Irish Book Award.

His short story *Everything in this Country Must*, directed by Gary McKendry, was filmed and was nominated for an Academy Award in 2005.

In May 2009 Colum became a member of Aosdána.

MY DUBLIN – COLUM MCCANN
'A puzzling city, a contradictory city, a terrible beauty of a place, up and down, high and low, riverrun, hillclad, sea-nestled, and maddeningly mysterious. But Dublin a city that has always allowed words to matter. Put any language you want on it, Dublin has been given oxygen by its stories. And Dublin listens well. It always has and always will.'

From *Let the Great World Spin*, Colum McCann
(Random House 2009)

All Respects to Heaven, I like it Here –

One of the many things my brother, Corrigan, and I loved about our mother was that she was a fine musician. She kept a small radio on top of the Steinway in the living room of our house in Dublin and on Sunday afternoons, after scanning whatever stations we could find, Radio Éireann or BBC, she raised the lacquered wing of the piano, spread her dress out at the wooden stool, and tried to copy the piece through from memory: jazz riffs and Irish ballads and, if we found the right station, old Hoagy Carmichael tunes. Our mother played with a natural touch, even though she suffered from a hand that she had broken many times. We never knew the origin of the break: it was something left in silence. When she finished playing she would lightly rub the back of her wrist. I used to think of the notes still trilling through the bones, as if they could skip from one to the other, over the breakage. I can still after all these years sit in the museum of those afternoons and recall the light spilling across the carpet. At times our mother put her arms around us both, and then guided our hands so we could clang down hard on the keys.

It is not fashionable anymore, I suppose, to have a regard for one's mother in the way my brother and I had then, in the mid-1950s, when the noise outside the window was mostly wind and sea chime. One looks for the chink in the armour, the leg of the piano stool shorter than the other, the sadness that would detach us from her, but the truth is we enjoyed each other, all three of us, and never so evidently as those Sundays when the rain fell gray over Dublin Bay and the squalls blew fresh against the windowpane.

Our house in Sandymount looked out to the bay. We had a short driveway full of weeds, a square of lawn, a black ironwork fence. If we crossed the road we could stand on the curved seawall and look a good distance across the bay. A bunch of palm trees grew at the end of the road. They stood, smaller and more stunted than palms elsewhere, but exotic nonetheless, as if invited to come watch the Dublin rain. Corrigan sat on the wall, banging his heels and looking over the flat strand to the water. I should have known even then that the sea was written in him, that there would be some sort of leaving. The tide crept in and the water swelled at his feet. In the evenings he walked up the road past the Martello Tower to the abandoned public baths, where he balanced on top of the seawall, arms held wide.

On weekend mornings we strolled with our mother, ankle-deep in the low tide, and looked back to see the row of houses, the tower, and the little scarves of smoke coming up from the chimneys. Two enormous red and white power station chimneys broke the horizon to the east, but the rest was a gentle curve, with gulls on the air, the mail boats out of Dun Laoghaire, the scud of clouds on the horizon. When the tide was out, the stretch of sand was corrugated and sometimes it was possible to walk a quarter-mile among isolated waterpools and bits of old refuse, long shaver shells, bedstead pipes.

Dublin Bay was a slow heaving thing, like the city it horseshoed, but it could turn without warning.

Denis Florence MacCarthy
1817-82

Denis Florence MacCarthy had his first poetry and essays published when he was just seventeen. They appeared in *The Nation* and the *Dublin Magazine*. He used the name 'Desmond' when he wrote on matters political. The house in which he was born in O'Connell Street (then Sackville Street) became the Imperial Hotel from whose balcony James Larkin addressed the crowds during the 1913 Dublin Lockout. It was completely destroyed during the Easter Rising in 1916 and has long since been replaced by Clery's department store.

MacCarthy studied for the priesthood at St Patrick's College, Maynooth before switching to law, which he never practiced. He lived at 74 Upper Gardiner Street, then at 38 Upper Baggot Street. He married and had nine children and lived in Summerfield in Dalkey, on the corner of the Old Quarry Road and Dalkey Avenue. He became the first professor of English Literature at the Catholic University which was situated in two of Dublin's finest Georgian houses, 85 and 86 St Stephen's Green.

He lived abroad for some years, but returned to Dublin to 28 Mount Merrion Avenue, Blackrock, where he died.

James Joyce put MacCarthy's *Poetical Works* beside Thom's *Dublin Post Office Directory* on Leopold Bloom's bookshelf in *Ulysses*.

During his life he translated some of the works of Pedro Calderón de la Barca from Spanish, including *The Purgatory of Saint Patrick* and wrote two biographies, *Poets and Dramatists of Ireland*,

and *Shelley's Early Life*. His poetry included *Irish Legends and Lyrics*, *The Bridal of the Year*, *Summer Longings* and a long narrative poem *The Voyage of St. Brendan*.

Donagh MacDonagh
1912-68

Poet, short story writer and playwright, Donagh MacDonagh was the son of executed patriot and poet Thomas. He attended Belvedere College and UCD, where amongst his peers were Brian O'Nolan, Cyril Cusack and Mervyn Wall. He lived at various addresses in Dublin: on Dartmouth Square, Rathmines as a student; at 33 Farney Park, Sandymount during his first marriage, and after some years on the legal circuit in the west he moved back to 141 Strand Road, Dublin.

His literary interests were broad and he edited the *Oxford Book of Irish Verse*, with Lennox Robinson. He published three volumes of poetry: *Veterans and Other Poems*, *The Hungry Grass* and *A Warning to Conquerors*. *Happy as Larry*, the play that was his most successful, has been translated into several languages.

Donagh MacDonagh is buried in Deansgrange Cemetery with his two wives, Maura and Nuala, both neé Smith.

Thomas MacDonagh
1878-1916

A meeting with Patrick Pearse on the Aran Islands, where MacDonagh and Pearse were learning the Irish language, led to him becoming the first teacher at Pearse's new school, St Enda's. Originally in Cullenswood House in Ranelagh, the school relocated to Rathfarnham where MacDonagh lived in the gate lodge while studying for his MA and BA degrees.

Prior to that he lived at 29 Oakley Road in Ranelagh. After graduation he joined the English Department in University College Dublin. His friends included Joseph Plunkett, Seumas O'Sullivan, WB Yeats, AE and James Stephens. By the time he married Muriel Gifford in 1912, his play *When the Dawn is Come* had been produced at the Abbey Theatre, and in 1914, along with Edward Martyn and Joseph Plunkett, he founded the Irish Theatre in Hardwicke Street. His play *Pagans* was produced there the following year. He never got to see his Ph.D. dissertation in print. This was *Literature in Ireland: Studies in Irish and Anglo-Irish*, which was published after his death. As one of the signatories of the 1916 Proclamation and as a garrison leader on Easter Sunday, he was sentenced to death and executed in Kilmainham Gaol. His body was buried in quicklime in the military cemetery at Arbour Hill. This is the last resting place of fourteen of the executed leaders of the insurrection. Among those buried there are his compatriot and friend, Patrick Pearse.

MacDonagh's other works include *April and May*, *The Golden Joy*, *Songs of Myself* and *Lyrical Poems*.

Micheál MacLiammóir
1899-1978

MacLiammóir chose that name over his more Anglo-sounding Alfred Willmore. Born in Cork, his parents moved to England when he was small and he became a child actor, making a name for himself playing roles like Peter Pan and Oliver Twist. But he hadn't lost his love of things Irish, and even after a period in Spain he was determined to learn to speak the Irish language fluently, which he did at the Gaelic League in London.

He came to Dublin in 1927 to act in the Intimate Shakespearean Company owned and run by Anew McMaster who was to become his brother-in-law when he married Micheál's sister Marjorie. Through him he met Hilton Edwards (1902-1982) and ever since the two names have been inextricably linked. They became lifelong partners in every sense of the word. In 1928 they produced the first play, Micheál's *Diarmuid agus Gráinne*, at *Taibhdhearc na Gaillimhe*, the Irish national language theatre based in Galway, and the same year they founded The Gate Theatre in Dublin. Both are still thriving.

The objective of their theatre was to fill the gaps being left by the homespun dramas playing out at the Abbey Theatre. Their vision was to introduce the audiences to works of a 'non-peasant' ilk, so their playbills saw names like Checkov, Strindberg, Cocteau, Ibsen, Shaw, Gabler and even some of MacLiammóir's own work feature. Above all the roles he played, and they were many over a long career, it is for his one-man show *The Importance of Being Oscar*, (*see poster above*) that he will always be remembered. He played this almost 1,400 times, and fittingly it was his last public appearance at the

Gate, in 1975, when he was seventy-six.

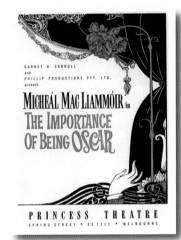

GARNET H. CARROLL and PHILLIP PRODUCTIONS PTY. LTD. present

MICHEÁL MAC LIAMMÓIR in THE IMPORTANCE OF BEING OSCAR

PRINCESS THEATRE
SPRING STREET • 32 1211 • MELBOURNE

Edwards and he lived at 4 Harcourt Terrace for thirty-four years and were both made a Freeman of Dublin City in 1973. They were also the subject of a biography by Christopher Fitz-Simon entitled simply - *The Boys*.

MacLiammóir predeceased Edwards by four years and they are buried in the same grave in St Fintan's Cemetery in Howth, County Dublin.

Conor McPherson
1971-

Playwright and screenwriter Conor McPherson was born in Dublin and studied in UCD where he wrote plays and directed them with a group of like-minded students. The Fly by Night Theatre Company developed when he left college. Some of his plays were produced in the International Bar in Wicklow Street and at the City Arts Centre on Moss Street City Quay (no longer there). Hailed by *The New York Times* as 'the finest playwright of his generation', Conor won the George Devine Award in 1997 for *St Nicholas*; an Olivier Award for Best New Play in 1999 with *The Weir*. In 2006 he received a Tony Award nomination for *Shining City* and an Olivier Award nomination for Best New Play for *The Seafarer*.

Aodhán Madden
1954-

Playwright, short story writer and poet, Aodhán Madden was educated by the Christian Brothers in North Brunswick Street and studied journalism at Rathmines College. He worked in the now defunct *Irish Press* Group as a sub-editor, feature writer and drama critic. His plays include *The Midnight Door*, *Sensations*, *Remember Mauritania*, and *Josephine in the Night*, which were all produced at the Peacock Theatre. He also had several productions over the years at the Dublin Theatre Festival.

He is thrice winner of the O Z Whitehead Award and thrice winner of the Francis MacManus Radio Short Story Competition and is a member of Aosdána.

In his much lauded 2009 novel *Fear and Loathing in Dublin* he draws on his own experiences of life as a newspaper sub, a gay and an alcoholic to portray yet another side of Dublin life.

DUBLIN CAN BE HEAVEN...
Dublin is both praised and criticised in many songs, not least in *The Dublin Saunter*, written by songwriter **Leo Maguire** 1903-85 for actor/singer **Noel Purcell** 1900-85 with whom it became indelibly linked. Purcell also recorded a talking version of Pete St John's *Dublin in The Rare Old Times*.

... IN THE RARE OLD TIMES
Pete St John or Peter Mooney as he was known at school in Synge Street, is a prolific composer of modern ballads His frequently recorded '*Dublin in the Rare Old Times*' could be classified as a tribute, a lament or a love song, or all three and more. In this ballad he hankers for what used to be: the things he had thought constant, but now gone. He regrets the passing of Nelson's Pillar and the Metropole Ballroom, two great symbols of old Dublin in O'Connell Street, as progress turned his town into a city - a strange place where 'glass cages' now line the River Liffey.

IN DUBLIN'S FAIR CITY...
So begins the ballad *Molly Malone*, about the legendary fishmonger whose bronze statue of her peddling her wares graces the pavement at the end of Grafton Street, opposite Trinity College. Sculpted by Jeanne Rynhart, it was erected to celebrate the Dublin millennium in 1988. The statue is known as 'The Tart With The Cart' or 'The Dish With The Fish'.

Bagatelle's 1980's song *Summer in Dublin* immortalised the 'young people walking on Grafton Street', the 46A bus and the River Liffey with its ability to make its presence felt 'as it stank like hell'.

James Clarence Mangan
1803-49

James Clarence Mangan was born at 5 Lord Edward Street, where his father had a failing spirit and grocery store. He lived a life of extreme poverty, during which he wrote copiously. For many, the poem they learned at school, *Dark Rosaleen*, is the work most connected with his name. Mangan lived in several city centre addresses: Chancery Street, York Street and Bride Street, and worked for a time in the library at Trinity College. He died of cholera in the Meath Hospital when he was just forty-three. William Stokes, one of the most distinguished physicians of the time, recognised him there and insisted he be given better care. In a biography of Stokes it is reported that Mangan said to him, 'You are the first person who has spoken a kind word to me for many years.' He died only a week or so after admission. In St Stephen's Green you'll find a bust of James Clarence Mangan, with an inset in the pedestal of *Róisín Dubh* or *Dark Rosaleen (see photo)*. It was unveiled in 1909 by Sir George Sigerson, President of the National Literary Society. In 1981 words from Mangan's most famous poem were inscribed on his headstone in Glasnevin Cemetery:

*Oh My Dark Rosaleen,
Do not sigh, Do
not weep.*

Sir John Pentland Mahaffy
1839-1919

A plaque marks the home of John Pentland Mahaffy at 38 North Great George's Street. Born in Switzerland, he went on to become the Provost of Trinity College, with an address at 1 Grafton Street. He also lived in Sutton, and at Howth, Co Dublin. He published numerous works across a range of subjects, some of which, especially those dealing with the 'Silver Age' of Greece became standard authorities. He is best remembered for his opposition to the revival of the Irish language and for being Oscar Wilde's tutor. Of the former he said that reviving the language 'would be a return to the Dark Ages.' Of the latter he was happy to take credit for teaching him 'the art of conversation'. They became close friends, but after the scandal, Mahaffy denied him, saying ,'We no longer speak of Mr Wilde.'

He is buried in St Fintan's Cemetery, Sutton, County Dublin. Part of his inscription reads, *He devoted his life to learning and to the education of his fellow countrymen.*

Edward Martyn
1859-1924

Born in the impressive Tulira Castle in Galway, but ending in a pauper's grave in Glasnevin in Dublin, Edward Martyn's life is fascinating. Monied and privileged, a patron of

Saint Mary's Pro-Cathedral

the arts and a fine musician, he spent a fortune restoring and renovating his family pile, only to live there like a hermit in a small room in its Norman tower, although he entertained lavishly, travelled extensively, collected art and played the organ as well as writing plays.

His neighbours were W B Yeats and Lady Gregory, whom he introduced, a meeting that would have far-reaching consequences. Martyn had written some plays by this time, *The Heather Field* and *Maeve*, and he was lamenting the fact that there was no theatre in Ireland to stage them. Over conversation one afternoon at Lady Gregory's Coole Park the notion of starting a theatre in Dublin was first mooted. The result was the Literary Irish Theatre, which opened in Dublin in 1899 in Hardwicke Street. The first two plays to be produced were Edward Martyn's *The Heather Field* and *The Countess Cathleen* by Yeats, followed by George Moore's *The Bending of the Bough*. Martyn funded the first three seasons of the theatre and although he remained life-long friends with Lady Gregory, he had a less amicable relationship with Yeats. He opposed the impending visit of Edward VII to Ireland and was

blackballed by The Kildare Street and University Club, of which he was a member. Martyn took them to court and was reinstated. By way of revenge he would kneel at one of the windows overlooking Nassau Street as the Angelus bells rang out from Westland Row church, and begin reciting the Rosary while people gathered outside to pray the responses. When asked why he stayed a member of the club, he famously replied that it was the only place in Dublin he could get caviar.

He founded the Palestrina Choir at Saint Mary's Pro-Cathedral with an endowment of £10,000. He suffered badly from arthritis in the last years of his life and spent these reclusively in Tulira. When he died it was learned with great surprise that he had stipulated that his body was to be donated for medical research and afterwards to be buried in the Poor Ground (paupers' graves) at Glasnevin Cemetery. He made his final journey with six other bodies in a workhouse van, the only distinguishing feature of his interment was the chanting of the *Benedictus Dominus Deus Meus* by his Palestrina Choir.

His other works include *'A Plea for a National Theatre in Ireland'*, *The Place-Hunters: A Political*

Comedy in One Act, *The Tale of a Town: A Comedy of Affairs*, and *An Enchanted Sea*.

Aidan Carl Mathews
1956-

Dublin-born poet, playwright and author, Aidan (Carl) Mathews was educated by the Jesuits at Gonzaga College and UCD. He got an MA from Trinity College Dublin. His career has included being a drama producer in radio and teaching English at St Louis High School, Rathmines, and Belvedere College. His poetry collections include *Windfalls*, *Minding Ruth* and *According to the Small Hours*. He has had *The Diamond Body* produced in the Project Theatre, and *Entrance*, *Exit* and *Communion* both at the Peacock. He also wrote a novel, *Muesli at Midnight*.

Charles Robert Maturin
1780-1824

Three Dubliners stand out as masters of horror, fear and good gothic suspense: Bram Stoker, Joseph Sheridan le Fanu and the Rev Charles Robert Maturin.

The earliest of these was Maturin, who lived in 37 York Street, and was a descendant of one of the many Huguenot families who fled to Ireland to avoid religious persecution in France. He was a curate in the local St Peter's Church in Aungier Street, a position he held all his life. He was known as a bit of an eccentric, a flamboyant dresser betimes, at others dressed like a 'charity case,' according to William Carleton who met him in Marsh's Library and visited him at his home. He was someone who loved dancing and could often be seen practising his steps through the windows of his home in York Street. Although he wrote several other novels, his gothic ones are best remembered. His contemporary, French novelist and playwright Honoré de Balzac, was reported to have been a great follower.

Maturin's central character was Melmoth the Wanderer, a half-man, half devil who had sold his soul to the devil in return for immortality. When we meet him he is already 150 years old and desperately trying to find someone to take over this pact from him. Maturin was the uncle of Jane Frances Elgee, later to become Jane Wilde the poet, better known as Speranza and Oscar Wilde's mother. When Oscar went into exile in France, following the scandals around his personal life, he chose the name of Sebastian Melmoth, from his granduncle's character.

Maturin was buried in St Peter's Church in Aungier Street. When the church was demolished in the 1980, to make way for the YMCA building, all the remains were re-interred in Mount Jerome Cemetery.

Paula Meehan
1955-

Poet and Aosdána member Paula Meehan was born in Gardiner Street and later lived in Finglas. She went to Trinity College and then attended Eastern Washington University where she took a MFA in Poetry. She has written numerous volumes of poetry, several plays, some for children. *The Wolf of Winter* was produced at the Abbey Theatre. Her latest poetry collection is *Painting Rain* (2009). Meehan has also written poetry for film and for contemporary dance companies. Scenes from her city childhood and the people who influenced her – her mother and grandmother – inspire much of her work. Her poem *Buying Winkles* from her collection *The Man Who Was Marked By Winter* recalls a forgotten Dublin where people bought their fish from fish sellers on the streets, and brought them home wrapped in newspaper.

Paul Mercier

Dublin playwright Paul Mercier was a teacher at Greendale Community School, Kilbarrack, where Roddy Doyle was also on the staff. Proving that there is life after the classroom, he founded the Passion Machine Theatre Company at 27 Mountjoy Square. He has received numerous awards: the Harvey's Irish Theatre Award for Best New Irish Work, The Sunday Independent Arts Award, The Rooney Prize for Irish Literature, and an Edinburgh Fringe First Award. His plays include *Studs*, *We Ourselves* and *Spacers*, in addition to *Homeland* and *Down The Line* for the Abbey Theatre. He also has written and directed three short films, *Before I Sleep*, *Lipservice* and *Tupperware*. His latest plays *The Passing* and *East Pier* featured in the Abbey Theatre's 2011 calendar.

George Moore
1858-1933

George Moore was born at Moore Hall in County Mayo. He was schooled in England and failed miserably as a student, eventually being expelled. His family moved to London and, spurning

WRITER
GEORGE MOORE
LIVED IN THIS HOUSE
1901-1911

the military career favoured by his father, George studied art, a path which led him to Paris. There he met many of the significant artists and writers of the time: Pissaro, Renoir, Monet, Degas, Emile Zola, Alphonse Daudet and the Russian writer Ivan Turgenev. He self published his first collection of poetry, but as with many subsequent writings, his treatment of subjects such as prostitution and lesbianism meant he fell foul of the establishment. He returned to Ireland in the 1880s to a country suffering the early stages of the Great Famine. He was perceived to be a very fair landlord, who didn't evict his tenants for their inability to pay rent. He abandoned art for writing and moved to London. His first novel *A Modern Lover* (1883) was banned. *A Mummer's Wife* and *A Drama in Muslin* were also banned. In 1886 he wrote a memoir of his twenties, entitled *Confessions of a Young Man.*

At the suggestion of his cousin, Edward Martyn, he returned to live in Dublin in 1901. He moved to 4 Ely Place where he managed to aggravate most of the neighbours (Oliver St John Gogarty and Bram Stoker's brother) in this gated community, especially when he painted his hall door a green colour, about which one of them lodged a

complaint. For revenge he used to run his cane along the railings to set the neighbourhood dogs yapping when everyone was asleep. In return they engaged a barrel organist to play outside his house when they knew he would be writing. He is reputed to have said that one of the perks of living at number 4 was that he had a perfect view of the nuns' underwear flapping in the breeze across the street in the Loreto Convent garden.

Moore's plays include *The Strike at Arlingford* and one co-written with Yeats called *Diarmuid and Grania.*

Thomas Moore
1779-1852

A plaque marks the spot at 12 Aungier Street where Thomas Moore was born, above his father's general merchants' providers store. He attended Samuel Whyte's Academy at 79 Grafton Street, now Bewley's Café. The partial repeal of the Penal Laws meant that Moore was one of the first Catholics to be allowed to attend Trinity College. While at Whyte's Academy he met and befriended patriot Robert Emmet, a friendship which endured until Emmet's execution in 1803, outside St Catherine's Church in Thomas Street.

Moore moved to England and was appointed Admiralty Registrar in

Statue of Thomas Moore on College Green

Bermuda. He married a sixteen-year-old actress, Bessy Dyke. They had six children, all of whom predeceased him, and their loss drove him to melancholy at times.

He travelled widely and although remembered now for his *Melodies* more than his prose, he wrote several fine biographies, including *The Life and Death of Lord Edward Fitzgerald* and *Letters and Journals of Lord Byron*, with *Notices of his Life* and *Memoirs of the Life of Richard Brinsley Sheridan*. Byron, whom he had first met in Venice, left him his papers, but on learning that his family didn't want them made public because of their frank revelations about his life and lifestyle, he burned them. Moore penned his *Melodies* to traditional tunes and many endure to this day. They were popular in drawing room recitals in their time and some are mentioned by Joyce in *Dubliners*. He was also given a monumental advance of £3000 for his poem *Lalla Rookh*, the story of a princess travelling from Delhi to Kashmir.

He is buried in England but is mentioned on his parents' and siblings' gravestone in St Kevin's churchyard, Camden Row, which is now a public park. It reads '… and their beloved daughter Ellen who died Feb 14th 1846, deeply mourned by her brother Thomas Moore, the bard of his much loved country Ireland.'

Among Moore's best-loved melodies are *The Last Rose of Summer*, *The Harp that once Through Tara's halls*, *Let Erin Remember*.

Lady Morgan
1776-1859

It was a quirk of fate that Sydney Owenson, later Lady Morgan, was considered Irish at all, for the story goes that she was born aboard the steam packet ship bringing her Irish actor father to Dublin, where he was scheduled to appear at the Theatre Royal in Crow Street. They must have had means because he then went on to set up his own company – in the Musik Hall in Fishamble Street, where Handel's *Messiah* premiered in 1742. When they lived in Drumcondra he was able to pay for private education for his daughters who boarded in Clontarf and then went to finishing school in Earl Street, where they were taught social graces. However, soon after this, their father was declared a bankrupt and Sydney became a governess and started writing novels. Her books were very popular at the time and include *The Wild Irish Girl*, *The Heiress of Desmond*, *The O'Briens and the O'Flaherty* and *The Novice of Saint Dominick*. In 1812 she married the philosopher and surgeon to the Abercorn household, Thomas Charles Morgan, who was afterwards knighted.

Val Mulkerns
1925-

Val Mulkerns was educated at the Dominican Convent in Eccles Street, the street where fictional Molly Bloom lived with Leopold in *Ulysses*. She left Ireland for a time and returned as associate editor of *The Bell* from 1952 to 1954. She was actively involved in the efforts of a band of writers who were trying to have censorship removed or at least applied logically. These included Sean O'Faoláin, Frank O'Connor and Peadar O'Donnell. Mulkerns had her first novel, *A Time Outworn*, published in 1951, followed by *A Peacock Cry* (1954), *The Summerhouse* (1984). She wrote short stories as well as two children's books, and is a regular broadcaster. She lived on Garville Road, Rathgar for over forty years, moving in 1996 to Dalkey to be beside the sea.

She is a member of Aosdána.

Iris Murdoch
1919-1999

Acclaimed novelist Iris Murdoch was born at 59 Blessington Street, Dublin, and although her family moved back to England when she was a child, she kept very strong bonds with her Irish relatives, spending holidays here and describing herself as Irish too. She wrote twenty-six novels. *The Red and the Green* is set against the backdrop of Dublin in the week before the Easter Rising of 1916, amid the complexities of families, Anglo Irish and Republican. Murdoch was awarded the Booker Prize in 1978 for *The Sea, the Sea*.

She suffered from Alzheimer's disease in the last years of her life, a journey that is catalogued in a film called simply *Iris* (2001) starring Judi Dench.

'One doesn't have to get anywhere in a marriage. It's not a public conveyance.' – A Severed Head

MAN BOOKER PRIZE WINNERS AND CONTENDERS

Iris Murdoch won in 1978 for *The Sea, The Sea*.
Jennifer Johnston's *Shadows on Our Skin* was shortlisted in 1977. Her *Old Jest* won in 1979.
Roddy Doyle's The Van was shortlisted in 1991 and in 1993 he won with *Paddy Clarke Ha Ha Ha*.

Paul Murray
1975-

Paul Murray's upbringing in South County Dublin and his attendance at one of the city's prestigious schools, Blackrock College, may well have given this author all the inspiration and material he needed to write *Skippy Dies*. He read English at Trinity College and worked at the now defunct Waterstones Bookstore in Dawson Street, where some of his books were launched. His first novel, *An Evening of Long Goodbyes*, was shortlisted for the Whitbread Prize in 2003 and nominated for the Kerry Irish Fiction Award at Listowel Writers' Week. *Skippy Dies* was long-listed for the Booker Prize and the Bollinger Everyman Wodehouse Award for Comic Fiction, both in 2010.

Tom Murphy
1935-

Born in County Galway, playwright Tom Murphy is now Dublin based. In 1961, *A Whistle in the Dark*, his first successful play, was staged at the Theatre Royal, Stratford East in London. Considered by many to be among our greatest living playwrights, in 2001 Murphy was honoured by the Abbey Theatre with a retrospective of six of his plays. His work includes *The Wake*, *The House*, *Bailegangaire*, *The Sanctuary Lamp*, *The Gigli Concert*, widely regarded as his masterpiece, *The Alice Trilogy*, and *The Last Days of a Reluctant Tyrant*. Murphy has written one novel, *The Seduction of Morality*. He is a member of the Irish Academy of Letters and of Aosdána.

TC Murray
1873-1959

Thomas Cornelius Murray was born in Macroom, County Cork. He trained at St Patrick's College in Drumcondra before returning to Cork to teach. When offered the headmastership of the Model School in Inchicore he moved back to Dublin and lived at 11 Sandymount Avenue. Murray had been writing and had his play *Wheel of Fortune* produced in the Little Theatre in Cork, which he co-founded. That success was quickly followed with another. When the Abbey agreed to produce *Birthright*, it was to herald a long association that would see a further fourteen of his plays running there. He also wrote *Aftermath*, *Autumn Fire*, *Michaelmas Eve* and perhaps his best one, *Maurice Harte*.

CARDINAL JOHN HENRY NEWMAN AND THE CATHOLIC UNIVERSITY OF IRELAND

Rev. John Henry Newman (1801-90) was a convert to Catholicism. Archbishop Cullen invited him to Dublin, expressly with the intention of setting up a Catholic University here. He met with much opposition at the time when he voiced his views on education in a series of lectures that he called *The Idea of a University* in 1852. He lodged in Dorset Street at this time and said daily Mass at St Xavier's Church in Gardiner Street, before moving to rooms in a boarding school at 16/17 Harcourt Street. His role as Rector of the Catholic University of Ireland was made official in June 1854 in a ceremony in St Mary's Pro-Cathedral, Marlborough Street. All that remained then was to find suitable premises. Charles Bianconi (of Bianconi Cars) one of the university committee, was given the charge of purchasing 86 St Stephen's Green, and the university was born. This later became known as Newman House. When it opened its doors in 1854 it had only seventeen students and an average of twenty-five per year for the next twenty or so years. Newman was adamant that the new establishment should have a medical school and a church. The odd-shaped piece of land between 86 and 87 was bought, on which was built a very elaborately decorated place of worship, which although called the University Church of Saints Peter and Paul, is simply referred to by Dubliners as University Church. The arrival of the Jesuits to open a school at St Stephen's Green coincided with a much greater influx of students.

Now known as University College Dublin, when it moved to its present campus at Belfield it took the original church bell from University Church with it. Newman House continues to be part of UCD and its magnificent rooms are open to the public at certain times. *University College Dublin Press* has its headquarters in the basement.

Twenty years after Newman returned to England he was made a Cardinal. He is buried in the grounds of the Oratory Fathers in Rednal, Birmingham. His best remembered writings are his hymn *Lead Kindly Light*, his poem *Dream of Gerontius* and his *Apologia pro Vita Sua*. He was beatified by Pope Benedict in England in 2010.

'To live is to change, and to be perfect is to have changed often' – John Henry Newman

Éilis Ní Dhuibhne
1954-

Éilís Ní Dhuibhne grew up in Walkinstown and was educated through Irish at Scoil Bhride and Scoil Chaitriona before attending UCD. David Marcus published her first short story, *Green Fuse*, on the 'New Irish Writing' page in the *Irish Press* in 1974. Marcus was something of a legend at spotting new talent and published many more of Éilís's stories over the next ten years. She once said that if he didn't like them she put them straight in the bin! Her first book was *Blood and Water*. She has since written several collections of short stories, many novels, children's books, poetry, and plays for stage and radio. Her work has won many awards including the Stewart Parker award for Drama, the Butler Award (American Association of Irish Studies) for Prose, several Oireachtas Awards for novels in Irish and three Bisto Awards for Children's Literature. Her novel, *The Dancers Dancing*, was shortlisted for the Orange Prize. Her short story collection, *The Pale Gold of Alaska*, was selected as a Notable Book of the Year by the *New York Times*. She is a member of Aosdána.

NEW IRISH WRITING AND DAVID MARCUS

Cork-born **David Marcus** **1924-2009** qualified as a barrister from Kings Inns in Dublin. He edited *Irish Writing* and *Poetry Ireland* before making a name for himself as the much-loved and revered editor of 'New Irish Writing' in the *Irish Press* newspaper. Through this weekly platform he discovered, fostered and encouraged new arrivals on the literary scene – writers such as John McGahern, Joe O'Connor, Anne Enright, Dermot Bolger, Neil Jordan and Eilis Ní Dhuibhne.

He edited over thirty anthologies of Irish short stories and poetry, and wrote several novels, including *A Land Not Theirs*, and *A Land in Flames* and his autobiography, *Oughtobiography - Leaves from the diary of a hyphenated Jew*.

David Marcus married writer **Ita Daly** whom he had published in 'New Irish Writing' and they lived in Garville Avenue, Rathgar.

Edna O'Brien
1930-

Like the characters in her *Country Girls* trilogy, Edna O'Brien came to Dublin from County Clare when she was just sixteen, to qualify as a licentiate from the Pharmaceutical College of Ireland. It soon became clear to her that writing was all she wanted to do and she began working for the *Irish Press*. The coming of age and sexual awakening of her girls was to prove too racy for Irish readers, whom, it seemed, needed to be protected from such revelations, so they were banned here, although the trilogy won the Kingsley Amis Award in the UK. In the face of fierce opposition to her writings, particularly from her mother who was shamed by the explicit content and her daughter's blasphemous references to anything Catholic, O'Brien moved to London and continued to write prolifically. She never really mended the rift with her mother, something she always regretted. Instead, undeterred, she produced more novels, short stories and three plays. She also wrote two biographies, *Byron in Love* and *James Joyce*. Joyce, she claims, had a great influence on her writings. Other works include the *House of Splendid Isolation* trilogy, *A Scandalous Woman and Other Stories*. In 2006 she was appointed Adjunct Professor of English Literature at UCD. In 2009 she was honoured with the Bob Hughes Lifetime Achievement Award at a special ceremony at the Irish Book Awards in Dublin.

Her son Carlo Gebler, is also a writer. (*see p54*)

Sean O'Casey
1880-1964

'All the world's a stage and most of us are desperately unrehearsed.'

Sean O'Casey was born at 85 Upper Dorset Street, the last of thirteen children. As a child he didn't have good health and a specialist recommended that he rest his eyes and not attend school. Although not from the tenements – his father was a caretaker so they had proper accommodation – he drew on the streets, the living conditions and the poverty that he had witnessed in the various neighbourhoods with which he was familiar when he came to write his plays.

When his father was invalided off work with a back injury the family moved to 9 Innisfallen Parade, and on his death when Sean was six, they moved to 20 Lower Dominick Street, now the home of the National Youth Federation. O'Casey finished formal schooling at fourteen and worked for nine years with the railway.

The family moved to nearby Abercorn Street, where he spent the next twenty-one years – the longest period he stayed anywhere in Ireland. He became interested in drama, due, he claims in his autobiography, *I Knock at the Door*, to the artistic endeavours of his brother Archie, who frequently put on plays in their crowded living space.

Around this time he also learned the Irish language, joined St Laurence O'Toole's Pipers Band in the Christian Brothers School on Seville Place, and became involved with the Irish Republication Brotherhood. He also became secretary of the Irish Citizen Army and a firm follower of 'Big' Jim Larkin, who had instigated the general strike that led to the Lockout in Dublin in 1913.

When his mother died, O'Casey lodged temporarily with a friend at 35 Mountjoy Square, believed to be the setting of his play *The Shadow of a Gunman*, and then to 422 South Circular Road where he wrote his greatest works. He was now writing fulltime and quickly produced *The Plough and the Stars*, *Juno and the Paycock* and *The Shadow of a Gunman*, often referred to as his 'Dublin trilogy'.

In February 1926 *The Plough and the Stars* premiered at the Abbey Theatre. A few days later there was rioting during the performance. W B Yeats, a director of the theatre, rebuked the audience: '*You have disgraced yourselves again. Is this to be an ever-recurring celebration of the arrival of Irish genius?... Dublin has once more rocked the cradle of genius. From such a scene in this theatre went forth the fame of Synge. Equally the fame of O'Casey is born here tonight.*'

That same year he received the British Hawthornden Prize for 'imaginary literature', met his Irish-born future wife in London and decided to leave Ireland. He married Eileen Reynolds Carey a year later and although he produced a large body of work subsequently none of it enjoyed the same degree of success as his earlier ones. The Abbey Theatre had rejected *The Silver Tassie*, something he never quite forgave them for.

He wrote several books under his Irish name, Seán Ó Cathasaigh, including *The History of the Irish Citizen Army*. His autobiography stretches over six volumes and his life story was made into a film called *Young Cassidy*, which featured Rod Taylor as O'Casey. His other works include *The Silver Tassie*, *The Bishop's Bonfire*, and *The Drums of Father Ned*.

Almost blind, he died in St Marychurch, Torquay, Devon and was cremated in Golder's Green Crematorium in London and his ashes scattered there.

Frank O'Connor
1903-66

Frank O'Connor is another writer who adopted Dublin as his home. He was born Michael Francis O'Donovan in Cork, left school at fourteen and went to the Technical School at night to learn typing and other skills. He credits Daniel Corkery, one of his teachers, with opening his mind to the marvels of language. O'Connor fell foul of the law for his republican beliefs and was arrested and incarcerated in

Gormanstown Military Camp. After completing his sentence he became a librarian. There followed stints in Sligo, Wicklow and Dublin, where he was introduced to AE, who encouraged O'Connor, as he had done with many other emerging writers, and published him in the *Irish Statesman*. He continued to submit short stories and essays after he was posted back to Cork. In 1929 he was appointed the first librarian to the newly opened Pembroke Library on Anglesea Road, Ballsbridge, the last library ever to be funded by the Carnegie Foundation.

He remained in Dublin until 1952, with the exception of a few years when he married and lived in Woodenbridge in Wicklow. By 1939 he had moved into journalism and broadcasting, had become a director at the Abbey Theatre and had resigned after an acrimonious row. Two of his plays were performed there: *In the Train* and *Moses' Rock*.

He moved into a rented house on 57, Strand Road, Sandymount. He loved walking along the strand and was a familiar figure in the neighbourhood. At this time he became the poetry editor of *The Bell*, which Sean O'Faoláin had founded in 1940. He almost rivals James Joyce when it comes to the number of addresses he occupied in the following few years before he eventually moved to Stillorgan, to Seafield Crescent. Always strapped for cash he decided to try his luck in America on the university lecture circuit. This proved a hugely successful move. In no time he was being published in journals and periodicals over there and he became a contributor to the *New Yorker.* During the next five years he returned often to Dublin, wintering here once at the Mespil Apartments on Sussex Road close to the Grand Canal. When he returned in 1950 he lived in the Court Apartments, Wilton Place, where he died in 1966.

At his funeral in Deansgrange Cemetery the graveside orations were given by a distinguished group of his peers, Patrick Kavanagh, Brendan Kennelly and Flann O'Brien among them.

O'Connor wrote countless short stories, two novels *The Saint and Mary* and *Dutch Interior*, two autobiographies - *An Only Child* and *My Father's Son* and a biography of Michael Collins called *The Big Fella.*

Joseph O'Connor
1963-

Joseph O'Connor was born in Glenageary, Co Dublin and went to UCD, an institution which features in the opening of his debut novel,

Cowboys and Indians. It was shortlisted for the Whitbread Prize. Among his other bestsellers are *Desperadoes*, *The Salesman* and *Inishowen.* He has won the Hennessy Writer of the Year Prize, the Miramax Ireland Screenwriting Award and the Macaulay Fellowship of the Irish Arts Council. His latest novel *Ghost Light* is based loosely on the life of the Dublin actress Molly Allgood (Máire O'Neill) and her relationship with playwright John Millington Synge.

Ulick O'Connor
1928-

Ulick O'Connor grew up in Rathgar, where he still lives. He was educated by the Holy Ghost Fathers in St Mary's College, Rathmines and then at UCD, where he studied law and philosophy, and became known as a keen sportsman. He practiced at the Bar before forsaking that to write. Over the years he has produced an eclectic body of work encompassing biography, Irish history, drama and poetry. He is celebrated for his biographies of Oliver St John Gogarty, Brendan Behan, and his work *The Irish Literary Revival.* His autobiography, *The Ulick O'Connor Diaries 1970-1981: A Cavalier Irishman* was published in 2001.

He is a member of Aosdána.

Nuala O'Faolain
1940-2008

Dubliner Nuala O'Faolain was a popular journalist and author who published two volumes of memoir, *Are You Somebody?* and *Almost There – the onward journey of a Dublin Woman*, and a history with commentary, *The History of Chicago May,* all of which made the *New York Times* Bestseller lists. She also wrote two novels – *My Dream of You* and *Best Love, Rosie*, which was published posthumously in 2009.

Sean O'Faoláin
1900-91

Cork-born Sean O'Faoláin didn't migrate to Dublin until he was almost forty, by which time he had *Midsummer Madness* and other stories published. He was prolific in his output of work that spanned travel books, a play, biographies, five volumes of short stories and much more. He founded *The Bell*, a literary periodical, which, from its offices at 14 O'Connell Street, gave many writers their first start. He lived in Knockaderry, Killiney and then at 17 Rosmeen Park. He received

M.A. degrees from the National University of Ireland and from Harvard University, was a Commonwealth Fellow from 1926 to 1928 and a Harvard Fellow from 1928 to 1929.

He was elected Saoi of Aosdána in 1986.

Both he and his wife Eileen, also a writer, donated their bodies to Trinity College for medical research.

Liam O'Flaherty
1896-1984

An Aran islander, Liam O'Flaherty (left) was a late arrival in Dublin, although he had spent a short time in Blackrock College and a year in UCD before joining the Irish Guards. Towards the end of the First World War he was invalided out and became interested in Communism. This phase lasted a few years when, disenchanted with politics, he left for London and began to produce his first novels. Within three years he had had *Thy Neighbour's Wife*, *The Black Soul*, and *The Informer* published as well a numerous short stories.

O'Flaherty became one of the founder members of the Irish

Academy of Letters. He travelled extensively, writing journals along the way and returned to settle in Dublin - in the Court Apartments, Wilton Place where Frank O'Connor had lived.

He set four of his novels amid the poverty and deprivation of 1920s Dublin: *The Insurrection*, *The Informer*, which won the James Tait Award and was made into a film of the same name in 1935, *The Assassin* and *The Puritan*, but it as a short story writer that he is best remembered. He also wrote three volumes of autobiography.

John O'Leary
1830-1907

A Tipperary man, John O'Leary was an active Fenian and editor of the *Irish People*. He attended Trinity College, studying law and then medicine, neither of which he completed. In 1865, O'Leary was charged with high treason and sentenced to twenty years penal servitude. He spent a number of years in English prisons, but, after an amnesty, went off to Paris, where he spent much of his time writing. He returned to Dublin in 1885 with his sister, the poet Ellen O'Leary, and they lived at 40 Leinster Rd, Rathmines. The house became a hub where writers, poets and

nationalists congregated. Frequent visitors were Katherine Tynan, Douglas Hyde, Thomas WH Rolleston and his sometimes adversary W B Yeats. Yeats asked his help when editing *Folk Tales of the Irish Peasantry*, *Stories from Carleton* and *Representative Irish Tales*. His sister's death saw John relocate to 134 Rathgar Road, and subsequently to 30 Grosvenor Road, then across the river to Mountjoy Square and 17 Temple Street. His collection of books numbered over 10,000 and his friends said he never chose his homes for their location but for their ability to house his treasures. He moved twice more, to Lonsdale House on St Laurence Road, Clontarf, where Yeats used to stay on his visits back to Ireland, and 11 Warrington Place.

O'Leary is buried in Glasnevin beside James Stephens, both graves marked with identical Celtic crosses. The plinth on O'Leary's is inscribed on all four sides with his sayings. One side reads,

Emmet desired that his epitaph be not written until his country was free. Strive with might and main to bring about the hour when his epitaph can be written, but I and all of you have much to do.

His memoirs were published as *Recollections of Fenians and*

Fenianism, His other works include *What Irishmen Should Know*, *Celtic Myths and Legends* and *The High Deeds of Finn Mac Cumhail*.

Brian O'Nolan (aka Flann O'Brien and Myles na gCopaleen) 1911-66

Brian O'Nolan always claimed to be a Dubliner, despite his Tyrone roots. The family moved where his father's work dictated and this pattern saw them living in Inchicore for a time, then in various parts of the country for several years. In 1921 the family settled in 25 Herbert Place. Brian and his brothers were sent to the CBS in Synge Street and later to Blackrock College. He went to UCD, where he enjoyed student life hugely and acquired an ample supply of material for his future writings, especially for *At Swim-Two-Bird*s. He partook enthusiastically of the banter and discourse in the local pub, Grogan's at the time – now O'Dwyer's on Leeson Street. He enjoyed stirring things up in the alternative college magazine *Comhthrom Féinne* for which he wrote under numerous pseudonyms, and became its editor in 1933. He started his own magazine *Blather*, which vanished without a trace after only a half dozen issues.

When he was just twenty-six his father died and Brian was faced with supporting ten siblings and his mother. This may explain why he stayed for eighteen years in the civil service, where he reached the rank of Ministerial Private Secretary. However, he continued to write to newspapers, submitting letters, essays, opinion pieces and short stories. For twenty-five years under the name Myles na gCopaleen he wrote his satirical columns *An Cruskeen Lawn* for *The Irish Times*

He married Evelyn McDonnell in 1948 and they moved to 8 Mount Merrion Avenue, where yet another persona emerged, this time as Stephen Blakesley, the author of several detective novels. Brian's ill health forced him to take early retirement from the service aged 42. This allowed him write full time and he produced *The Hard Life*, *An Béal Bocht* and *The Dalkey Archive*. The latter was dramatized by Dalkey playwright Hugh Leonard for the Dublin Theatre Festival in 1965 under the title *The Saints Go Cycling In*.

News of Brian's death was announced on April Fool's Day, 1966, but as he was known for his quirky sense of humour many of his friends initially believed this was yet another prank. He is buried in the family grave in Deansgrange Cemetery.

His best known work, *The Third Policeman*, written in 1939/40, was published posthumously. *The Brother,* a stage show by Eamonn Morrissey, was based on the writings of Flann O'Brien.

Mark O'Rowe
1970-

Mark O'Rowe was born in Dublin and grew up in Tallaght. His hugely successful play *Howie the Rookie* won the George Devine Award, the Rooney Prize for Irish Literature and an Irish Times/ESB Irish Theatre Award for Best New Play in 1999. He was appointed joint writer-in-association at the Abbey Theatre for the 2004 centenary. The Abbey's 2007 production of his *Terminus* went on to win an Edinburgh Fringe First in 2008.

Siobhán Parkinson
1954-

Siobhán Parkinson was appointed Ireland's first **Laureate na nÓg**, or Children's Laureate, a position that will be awarded every two years to a distinguished

writer or illustrator of children's books in Ireland. The role was set up by the Arts Council in 2010 'to engage young people with high quality children's literature and to underline the importance of children's literature in our cultural and imaginative life.' Parkinson grew up in Galway and Donegal, but has lived in Dublin for many years. A graduate of Trinity College Dublin, her books for young readers have been translated into Danish, German, French, Italian, Spanish, Russian, Latvian, Lithuanian, Serbian, Bosnian, Slovenian, Thai, Japanese, Brazilian Portuguese, Mandarin Chinese. She's no stranger to getting awards and among her twenty books are the prize-winning *Sisters - No Way!*, *Amelia*, *The Love Bean*, *Breaking the Wishbone* and *Four Kids, Three Cats, Two Cows, One Witch (Maybe)*.

MY DUBLIN – SIOBHAN PARKINSON

When we drove into Dublin, home on holidays from our various places of exile in my childhood, I would get so emotional about the city that I used to imagine the car was hugging the streets, and I wanted to leap out and do the same. That visceral love of my native city has remained with me all my life, and it is (mostly) in Dublin's accents that my characters speak and it is through Dublin's streets (even when it isn't really) that they thread their enchanted lives.

Patrick Pearse
1879-1916

Dublin playwright, poet, writer and patriot, Patrick Henry Pearse (also Padraic Pearse) was executed for his part in the Easter Rising 1916. He was born at 27 Great Brunswick Street, (now called Pearse Street), before the family moved to Newbridge Avenue in Sandymount. He was educated by the Christian Brothers in Cumberland Street South, where he developed a love of the Irish language. Although he had studied law he wanted to start a school that taught through the medium of Irish – hence the birth of Scoil Éanna, or St Enda's, at Cullenswood House, Chelmsford Road in Ranelagh in 1908. This later moved to Rathfarnham and there are now two Gaelscoileanna in the original estate. The school in Rathfarnham closed in 1935 and is now the Pearse Museum.

Despite his active involvement in school and in the Republican movement, Pearse produced quite a volume of writings. He wrote four plays, *Íosagán*, *The Master*, *The King* and *The Singer*, three of which were produced by the Abbey Theatre, numerous stories and poems.

He was executed at Kilmainham Gaol the day before his brother, Willie, for their part in the Rising and they are buried in the

The General Post Office, Dublin, occupied by Pearse and his comrades during the 1916 Rising churchyard of the Church of the Sacred Heart, Arbour Hill.

Their fate fulfilled the sentiments of his poem

The Mother
I do not grudge them:
Lord, I do not grudge
My two strong sons
that I have seen go out
To break their strength and die, they and a few,
In bloody protest for a glorious thing,
They shall be spoken of among their people,
The generations shall remember them,
And call them blessed;
But I will speak their names to my own heart
In the long nights;
The little names that were familiar once
Round my dead hearth.
Lord, thou art hard on mothers:
We suffer in their coming and their going;
And tho' I grudge them not, I weary, weary
Of the long sorrow - And yet I have my joy:
My sons were faithful, and they fought.

Peter Pearson
1955-

Few people have captured the essence of their city like artist and writer Peter Pearson, who was born in Monkstown, Co Dublin. He has devoted much of his life to saving and preserving its essence and historic heart, recording images of the changing city in both his paintings and his writing. His works include *Dun Laoghaire–Kingstown*, *Between the Mountains and the Sea*, *The Heart of Dublin*, *Dublin's Victorian Houses*, *The Forty-foot, a monument to sea bathing* and *Decorative Dublin*.

For some years he and his family lived in the Sick and Indigent Roomkeepers Society building, on Palace Street, almost opposite the Olympia Theatre. He now lives in Wexford.

Paul Perry
1972-

Poet Paul Perry was born in Dublin. He grew up on Sandyford Road, Dundrum and went to St Killian's German School in Roebuck. He attended Brown University, Rhode Island and Trinity College, Dublin and now lives in Rathfarnham.

His first book of poetry *The Drowning of the Saints* was published in 2003 to critical acclaim and was shortlisted for the Rupert and Eithne Strong Award for Best First Collection at the Poetry Now Festival in Dun Laoghaire, Co Dublin. It was subsequently awarded The Listowel Prize for Poetry. He has also written collections called *The Orchard Keeper* and *The Last Falcon*.

James Plunkett
1920-2003

Dubliner James Plunkett Kelly, who preferred to be known simply as James Plunkett, was a playwright, short story writer and novelist. He was also an award-winning TV producer with RTÉ. He grew up in Sandymount and was educated at Synge Street CBS and at the Municipal School of Music in Camden Street, where he played the violin and the viola. On taking a position as a clerk in the Dublin Gas Company he became involved in the trade union movement, later becoming a full-time official. This brought him into contact with Jim Larkin, who was to become a major character in a radio play called *Jim Larkin* and in his novel *Strumpet City*. In

the mid-1950s Plunkett joined Radio Éireann (now RTÉ) as a drama assistant and began his career with a series of radio plays. In 1961 he was appointed one of the first two directors of the new national television station. *Strumpet City*, which is set amid the working classes in the years leading up the Dublin Lockout in 1913, was first published in 1969, and became his best loved work, as well as one of RTÉ's most successful drama series ever. It starred Peter O'Toole and Cyril Cusack. Some of his short stories were published in a collection called *The Trusting and the Maimed* and he was a member of Aosdána.

His remains were cremated at Mount Jerome Cemetery, Harold's Cross.

Joseph Plunkett
1887-1916

Poet and patriot Joseph Mary Plunkett was executed for his part in the 1916 Rising. His father, James, was a Papal Count, a bibliophile, journalist and barrister, who had once edited his own magazine called *Hibernia*. He gave his son a Jesuit education at Belvedere College in Great Denmark Street and at Stonyhurst in England and when he returned to Dublin he had private tutoring in Irish, given by Thomas MacDonagh. He lived in Larkfield in Kimmage and attended UCD. He helped Padraic Colum set up the new *Irish Review*, which he was later to edit along with James Stephens and Thomas MacDonagh. It didn't survive very long because of the subversive nature of some of its content, not least some items written by Plunkett himself, but while it lasted it published some of the best writers of the day. At this time too Plunkett made regular appearances on the pages of the *Irish Freedom* newspaper. He was also involved with setting up the Irish National Theatre with Edward Martyn, among others. This was located in Hardwicke Street, and its aim was to counteract 'the peasant drama' being staged at the Abbey!

His volume *The Poems of Joseph Mary Plunkett* was published posthumously. His only other collection *The Circle and the Sword* was published in 1911 on his return from travelling extensively in Europe and Egypt – journeys he had made to try and cure him of the tuberculosis that had plagued him since he was young.

He was one of the signatories of the Proclamation of Independence on Easter Sunday 1916 and was executed in Kilmainham Gaol on 4 May. He married his fiancée, Grace Gifford, in the chapel in the gaol (*see photo below*) only hours beforehand. He is buried along with other executed leaders of the Rising in the graveyard of the Church of the Sacred Heart, Arbour Hill. His best-remembered poem is *I See His Blood Upon the Rose*:

I see His blood upon the rose
And in the stars the glory of His eyes,
His body gleams amid eternal snows
His tears fall from the skies...

A DIP INTO SOME OF DUBLIN'S LITERARY PUBS

Dublin is a city of pubs, some more popular than others, but each with its set of regular patrons – from the student fraternity, the legal and political corps, the literary and theatrical crowd, musicians, tourists or the local Dublin 'man on the street'.

Several of the establishments around the city centre began being referred to as literary pubs because writers, journalists and poets tended to congregate in them. In certain watering holes they congregated to bounce ideas off each other, to drown their sorrows after yet another rejection letter from a paper or publisher or to celebrate a success, no matter how minor. Brendan Behan was known to bring his typewriter into McDaid's and work away, cautioning the other drinkers not to spill their pints anywhere near him. James Joyce mentions many hostelries in his writings about Dublin, and no self- respecting director films in this town without featuring some of the more atmospheric watering holes.

You can join in a Literary Pub Crawl, starting at the Duke in Duke Street, and meandering through the neighbouring streets, while being entertained by quotes and anecdotes pertaining to the various stops from Beckett, Joyce, Flann O'Brien, Behan, Kavanagh etc. or you might prefer to go walkabout and discover your own favourite.

While plasma screens, karaoke, match nights and live music have changed the scene in many of the places mentioned, you'll still find a snug or two, a quiet corner and maybe even a writer making notes on the back of an envelope or on a MacBook Pro.

The Brazen Head, on Bridge Street, Dublin 8 is immortalised in the words of Corley in Joyce's *Ulysses*. He recommends it in an understated way when he says, 'you can get a decent enough do at the Brazen Head for a bob' (a shilling!). Its liquor license dates back to 1668. However Corley may have had one too many by that stage as he got the address wrong in the book!

The Stag's Head, 1 Dame Court, was frequented by Joyce and is one of Dublin's truly unspoiled Victorian pubs, despite changing hands again in recent years. Its claim to fame is that it was one of the earliest pubs to be illuminated by electricity, but that's its nod to modernity, all the rest is true

vintage. Because of its proximity to the Gaiety and Olympia Theatres it's something of a 'local' for cast members and producers too. The premises starred in 'Educating Rita', which was filmed around Trinity College with Michael Caine and Julie Walters.

The Bleeding Horse on Camden Street dates back to 1649 and is still something of a landmark in the area. It attracted names like Joyce, Le Fanu, Gogarty and JP Donleavy, who all drank here.

Grogans, 15 South William Street, has stained glass at the back of the bar depicting literary icons such as Brendan Behan, Patrick Kavanagh,

Benedict Kiely, Michael Hartnett, Macdara Woods, Anthony Cronin and Liam O'Flaherty, who all supped here. Although it has its licence since 1899, credit is often given to a former barman in McDaid's for bringing the literati with him when he changed jobs in 1972. Many of these were regarded among the 'flight of the faithful' that followed Paddy O'Brien to Grogans.

In *At Swim–Two–Birds*, Flann O'Brien wrote 'We sat in Grogans with our faded overcoats finely disarrayed on easy chairs in the mullioned snug.'

McDaids, 3 Harry Street (*photo opposite*) was the 'in' place for scribes and poets until it lost Paddy O'Brien (*see above*), who had pulled many a pint and measured many a chaser for Behan, Kavanagh, O'Nolan et al. It is said that Behan based some of his characters in *The Hostage* and *Borstal Boy* on publicans he met in McDaid's. It's still a very popular and atmospheric place to visit, with its dark wood and Victorian interiors. You'd never know it had been a morgue previously!

O'Neill's, 2 Suffolk Street, is very a modern day meeting house for Trinity students and philosophers, as well as some of its dons. Brendan Kennelly, Professor of Modern

Interior of McDaids

Literature until 2005, regularly held court here, attended by a devoted coterie of his students.

Mulligan's, Poolbeg Street (above), was known as the 'sub office' by journalists of the *Irish Press*, which until its demise in 1995 was located next door. Many a headline and colour piece was penned 'under the influence' here. One of its favourite regulars was the legendary Con Houlihan, a Kerry journalist with the *Irish Press* who could turn any sporting event into a work of literature and erudition. His advice to journalism students was: 'Get two dictionaries - one to keep at home and one to keep in your pocket. Whenever you meet a new word,

shake salt on its tail and put a mark by its side in your dictionary.' His Kerry compatriots, poet Brendan Kennelly and playwright John B Keane, erected a plaque to him in this pub.

The Oval, 78 Middle Abbey Street, was a popular haunt with the press packs from the *Freeman's Journal*, the *National Press* and later from the *Independent Newspapers Group*

until it relocated. This bar is mentioned by Beckett in *More Pricks than Kicks*; it's also on Stephen Dedalus' and Ned Lambert's beat in *Ulysses*.

The Flowing Tide, 9 Lower Abbey Street is across the road from the Abbey Theatre and it offered refuge to many of the capital's playwrights and actors, as well as aspiring writers. It was also where patrons fled when riots broke out in protest at the 'immorality' and 'indecency' in JM Synge's *Playboy of the Western World* in 1907. It is now regarded as an authentic bit of 'auld Dublin'.

The Parnell Mooney was a favourite with Brendan Behan (he had a few of them, it seems!) and his cousin playwright Seamus (Jimmy) de Burca, who was born across the street in the Rotunda Hospital. Some of de Burca's plays were staged at the Gate Theatre. His work includes *Mrs. Howard's Husband*, *The Boys and Girls are Gone* and a novel, *Limpid River*.

Patrick Conway's on the corner of Moore Lane and Parnell Street was established in 1745 and closed in 2008. It's now derelict. It was historic for many reasons, not least because Republican

writer and poet Patrick Pearse surrendered outside its doors, but also for its starring role as a location in the film of Roddy Doyle's *The Snapper*.

Davy Byrne's, 21 Duke Street, is one of Dublin's best known pubs. Its clientele over the years has been eclectic, often eccentric and certainly a very literary bunch. It is here that Leopold Bloom in *Ulysses* asked for a Gorgonzola sandwich and a glass of Burgundy and where Joycean lovers still come in pilgrimage to congregate on *Bloomsday* (16 June) to demand the same. The décor is unique, with murals showing the faces of many well-known patrons at the time. These were painted by Cecil ffrench Salkeld, Behan's

father-in-law. Regulars included Behan, of course, Beckett, Oliver St John Gogarty, Flann O'Brien, Patrick Kavanagh and James Stephens.

The Duke, 9 Duke Street, dates back to 1882, and over the decades it became a second home to many of Dublin's native and adopted luminaries as well as would-be

scribes and poets. There's a framed collage of many who made it into literary Dublin lore. It's also the keeper of a letter penned in Paris by Joyce in 1926 in which he wrote home to announce that his '*Gens de Dublin*' (*Dubliners*) was now in its eight edition. This was written to his patron Harriet Shaw Weaver who had first serialised *A Portrait of the Artist as a Young Man* in *The Egoist* in 1914. Although estranged in later life, she paid for his funeral.

The Bailey 2-3 Duke Street, is a legend of its own making. Stories, apocryphal and otherwise, abound, and if the bar's tops and stools, the snugs and mirrors could talk they'd have some tales to tell. They'd recall the literary debates, the visits by the likes of John Betjeman and Evelyn Waugh, the raucous and opinionated rants by Trinity students and the liquid remedies for writer's block that went down so well here.

One story has it that Brendan Behan claimed that he had once bought the pub at an auction, mistakenly and almost certainly through an alcoholic haze, bidding for it instead of an electric toaster! He also amended the final draft of J P Donleavy's *The Ginger Man* for him in these hallowed surroundings, making his notes in the margins of Donleavy's pages.

Every year on Bloomsday this venue is frequented by Joycean scholars and followers, many dressed in striped blazers, straw boaters and elegant period gowns of the early 1900s. They gather here to remember Leopold Bloom and eat a commemorative breakfast based on the one described in *Ulysses*, and which always includes '*grilled mutton kidneys*', hopefully without the '*tang of faintly scented urine*'.

Doheny & Nesbitts, 4-5 Lower Baggot Street, has been a favourite over the years with journalists and politicians alike. Despite the fact that it lost a lot of its journalists when the *Sunday Tribune* relocated to the city centre, it still attracts the news hounds from the nearby Government Buildings who meet to discuss the latest political scandals and debacles. On Bloomsday 1904 these premises were the site of Delahunty's Tea and Wine Merchants.

Toner's, 139 Lower Baggot Street, enjoys the reputation of being the only pub ever to have been visited by WB Yeats. That fact is certainly debateable but the story goes that, in conversation with Gogarty, who lived around the corner in Ely Place, he mentioned that he had never been in a pub. Gogarty set about remedying this dreadful omission in the writer's life and brought him to Toner's, where instead of appreciating the Victorian ambience and passing a pleasant hour or two, after imbibing one modest sherry that Gogarty bought him, he declared that he wasn't impressed, and they left.

Farrington's is at 27-29 East Essex Street, Temple Bar, where it meets Eustace Street. It's called after Farrington, one of the characters in Joyce's story *Counterparts* in *Dubliners*, although it was called J.J. O'Neills in the book. It's now frequented by emerging and established playwrights and by the cast who take part in the readings and productions at the New Theatre, further along at number 43. This has its foyer in the Connolly Bookshop.

The Palace Bar, 1 Fleet Street, is most famous as the meeting place of a small coterie of significant figures in literary Dublin in the 1940s and 50s. It was something of an unofficial private club chaired by the famous editor of *The Irish Times* back then, Robert Smyllie. He was every caricaturist's dream – a portly man given to wearing a large felt hat and a poncho. In later life he swapped the hat for a beret. He cycled everywhere, often with his typewriter attached to the crossbar of his bike. His select company at his daily rendezvous could include John Betjeman, Brinsley McNamara, Patrick Kavanagh and Austin Clarke. These were frequently joined by Flann O'Brien, whom Smyllie had engaged to write a thrice-weekly column *Cruiskeen Lawn* under the pseudonym Myles na Gopaleen.

Deirdre Purcell
1945-

Dubliner Deirdre Purcell had been a newsreader, journalist and an acclaimed Abbey actress before turning to novel writing. She has produced an impressive and ever growing list of titles, including *A Place of Stones*, *Children of Eve*, *The Secret* and *Somewhere in Between*. Her *Follow Me Down to Dublin* is a non-fiction work packed with interviews and memories of a Dublin of bygone years.

Lennox Robinson
1886-1958

Cork-born Lennox Robinson became interested in drama and theatre after seeing the Abbey on tour at the Cork Opera House in 1907. Within two years he had his first play produced by the same company at the Abbey Theatre in Dublin, and with a three-month long run too. It was called *The Clancy Name*. This was followed shortly afterwards by *The Cross Roads*.

He made such an impression on Lady Gregory and Yeats that they engaged him as Play Director and Manager of the

Abbey and sent him to London to study his art. There he met and worked with names like Boucicault and Shaw. Apart from a short spell during WWI, he was to spend the rest of his life as a director of the board of the theatre.

He wrote twenty-one plays, a book on the theatre, two volumes of memoirs and some poetry, and also left his mark by founding the Abbey School of Acting.

He is buried in St Patrick's Close, beside St Patrick's Cathedral, next to Denis Johnston.

Patricia Scanlan
1956-

Patricia Scanlan was born in Ballygall and attended the Dominican Convent in Eccles Street. She joined the library service and was sent to the newly opened Ballymun Library, where she helped with an outreach programme that saw her fill her car with 'over fifty books and a trolley which I used to haul up flights of stairs and back down again, to unload and put back in the boot.' Scanlan had her first novel published in 1990, heralding a new wave of popular Irish contemporary women's fiction and putting her in the bestseller lists countless times. Many of her books are set in the Dublin she knows so well – The *City Girls* series, *Apartment 3B*, *Finishing Touches*, *Forgive and Forget* and *Coming Home*.

POPULAR CONTEMPORARY WOMEN'S FICTION WRITERS. Following the success of Maeve Binchy, Patricia Scanlan and Deirdre Purcell, a new wave of women writers emerged on the Dublin scene. These include Sheila O'Flanagan who gave up her job in financial trading to write; Patricia O'Reilly, lecturer, playwright and documentary maker; Anita Notaro, television producer and journalist; Claudia Carroll, actress and former *Fair City* soap star; journalist Cathy Kelly, Martina Devlin, and Cecelia Ahern whose debut novel *P.S. I Love You* was made into a movie.

Michael Scott
1959-

Dubliner Michael Scott began writing over twenty-five years ago, and is one of Ireland's most prolific authors, with one hundred titles to his credit, spanning a variety of genres, including fantasy, science fiction and folklore. He writes for both adults and young readers and is published in thirty-seven countries, in twenty languages. He is considered one of the authorities on the folklore of the Celtic lands and his collections, *Irish Folk and Fairy Tales*, *Irish Myths and Legends* and *Irish Ghosts & Hauntings* have remained in print for the past twenty years.

Scott's series *The Secrets of the Immortal Nicholas Flamel* has garnered ten literary award nominations, and *The Alchemyst* won the 2008 Rhode Island Book Award (Teens).

George Bernard Shaw
1856-1950

Regarded by many as one of our greatest and most prolific playwrights, George Bernard Shaw was born at 3 Upper Synge Street, Dublin, now 33 Synge Street. His mother, a singer better known as Hilda, sang regularly at the Antient Concert Rooms in Great Brunswick Street, now Pearse Street, and her music tutor, George Vandaleur Lee, was very much part of the Shaw household.

George didn't distinguish himself academically, spending some time at the Wesleyan Connexional School at 94 St Stephen's Green and then the Central Model Boy's School in Malborough Street, but not making much of an impression in either.

When his mother and sisters followed Mr Vandaleur Lee to London, George stayed behind with his father, attending the Dublin Scientific and Commercial Day School in Aungier Street. He got his first position with the land agents Charles Uniacke and Thomas Townshend, 15 Molesworth Street, where he progressed to chief cashier. George became a regular concert and theatregoer and was a frequent visitor to the National Gallery of Ireland in Merrion Square. In recognition of the pleasure these visits gave him, when he died he left a third of his posthumous royalties to the National Gallery. These escalated considerably with the enormous and continuing global success of the musical *My Fair Lady* (based on his play *Pygmalion*).

Shaw left Ireland in 1876, and wrote five novels in the next nine years, none of which was a success, although they were all published at later stages. In 1895 as a member of the Fabian Society he became one of the founders of

OUR NOBEL LAUREATES FOR LITERATURE

Since 1901 Nobel Prizes have been awarded to writers whose work has made 'an outstanding contribution' to various disciplines, including literature.

William Butler Yeats, poet and playwright, was the first Irish winner in 1923. The citation read: 'For his always inspired poetry, which gives expression to the spirit of a whole nation'.

He was a co-founder of Ireland's National Theatre, the Abbey. His son, Michael, said of his father, 'We were very aware that we were living with a national treasure.'

His works include *The Wild Swans at Coole*, *In The Seven Woods*, *The Wanderings of Oisin*, *The Land of Heart's Desire*, *Cathleen Ní Houlihan*, *Responsibilities: Poems and A Play*, *Baile and Aillinn* and *Crossways*.

Two years later, in 1925, another Dubliner, dramatist **George Bernard Shaw** was given the Nobel Prize in Literature. Although he moved to England where he married and settled down, he was fiercely proud of being an Irishman. Shaw turned down the monetary part of the Nobel Prize, requesting it be used to finance translation of Swedish books to English.

His plays include: *Man and Superman*, *Pygmalion*, *Saint Joan*, *Arms and the Man*, *The Doctor's Dilemma*, *John Bull's Other Island* and *Widowers' Houses*. Shaw is the only person to have been awarded both a Nobel Prize for Literature and an Oscar (1938) which he received for his work on the film of *Pygmalion*.

In 1969 **Samuel Beckett**, dramatist and poet, was the third native of the capital city to take the Nobel Prize in Literature. Although he lived most of his life in Paris, the Dublin of his childhood and youth featured in many of his writings, like *More Pricks than Kicks*. *Malone Dies*, *Dream of Fair to Middling Women* and *Molloy*. He also wrote *Waiting for Godot*, *Krapp's Last Tape* and *Endgame*.

Whilst in no way making poet **Seamus Heaney**, Ireland's fourth Noble Literature prizewinner, disinherit his Northern Ireland heritage to claim him as one of our own – he did chose to come and live and work in Dublin, where he now lives in Sandymount, so we welcome him among our three genuinely Dublin laureates with pleasure.

He won the award in 1995. His works include *Death of a Naturalist*, *Eleven Poems*, *The Haw Lantern*, *Door into the Dark*, *Station Island*, *District & Circle* and *Human Chain*.

the London School of Economics. He met his wife, Charlotte Payne-Townshend and they moved to Ayot St Laurence in Hertfordshire where he did all his writing in a revolving wooden hut at the end of the garden. That house is now in the hands of the National Trust and is known as Shaw's Corner. He lived there until his death, aged 94.

The Shaw birthplace in Dublin is now preserved as a museum and marked by a plaque that states, 'Author of Many Plays'. This simple accolade doesn't say that he was a winner of the Nobel Prize for Literature 1925, and an Oscar (for *My Fair Lady*). He was made a Freeman of Dublin in 1946.

He was cremated in Golder's Green Crematorium and his ashes were scattered with those of his wife in his gardens at Ayot St Laurence. Among his other works are *Man and Superman*, *John Bull's Other Island*, *The Doctor's Dilemma*, *The Devil's Disciple*, *Methuselah*, *Heartbreak Hotel* and *The Man of Destiny*.

Richard Brinsley Sheridan
1751-1816

It would have been difficult for young Richard Brinsley Sheridan, who was born at 12 Dorset Street, to avoid literary talent. His grandfather was a friend of Dean Swift, who was godfather to Richard. His father owned the Smock Alley Theatre in Smock Alley, now West Essex Street. His mother, Frances, was a playwright and a novelist. Richard went to school at Whyte's Academy in Grafton Street, where Thomas Moore and Robert Emmet were pupils. The family moved to London and Richard spent five unremarkable years at Harrow and then had private tutoring when his mother died. In 1773 he married Elizabeth Linley, a singer.

His play *The Rivals* had a shaky first night at Covent Garden in 1775, but then became very successful. The comic opera, *The Duenna*, was also a big hit and Sheridan became a partner at the Drury Lane theatre, and later the owner of the Theatre Royal, Drury Lane. In 1777 he wrote *The School for Scandal*, his most famous play and considered one of the greatest comedies of manners in English.

Sheridan stopped writing plays when he became a Member of Parliament, but his speeches there became known for their wit and oratory. He failed to be re-elected to Parliament in 1812, and his last years were spent in debt.

He was given a magnificent funeral in Westminster Abbey and is buried there in Poet's Corner.

In 1825 Thomas Moore published a two-volume biography *Memoirs of the Life of Richard Brinsley Sheridan*.

John D Sheridan
1903-80

John Desmond Sheridan was a novelist, short story writer and humourist, well remembered for his regular contributions to the *Irish Independent* newspaper. He wrote novels, essays and poetry as well as a biography of James Clarence Mangan. His novels include *Paradise Alley* and *The Rest is Silence*.

He is best remembered for his humorous work, and his poems, such as *'Joe's No Saint'* would have been regularly recited as 'party pieces'.

Jim Sheridan
1949-
and
Peter Sheridan
1952-

Brothers Jim and Peter Sheridan grew up in Seville Place, D1 and went on to make their mark on stage and film as well as in print. Although now associated mainly with movies, six- time Oscar nominee Jim's earlier work was in theatre. His plays include *Journal of a Hole* (co-authored with Peter Sheridan) and *The Ha'Penny Place*. His screen writing and screen director credits include *My Left Foot*, based on the life of Christy Brown, which got him an Oscar nomination for Best Director. *The Field*, *In the Name of the Father* and *The Boxer* are some of his best-known works. He lives in LA and on Coliemore Road in Dalkey.

Peter Sheridan's CV is equally impressive. He was one of the founder members of the Project Arts Centre. He has worked with Charabanc Theatre Company and the Royal Court Theatre where he directed his own plays, *The Liberty Suit* and *Emigrants*. Sheridan wrote and directed *The Breakfast*, a short film which won the Prix Arte Europe Award at the Brest International Film Festival. He also wrote and directed the film *Borstal Boy*, based upon Brendan Behan's memoir. He is the author of *44 – A Dublin Memoir* and another memoir *Forty-Seven Roses*.

Paul Smith
1920-97

Dublin-born playwright Paul Smith left school early and began working at both the Abbey and Gate Theatres in costume and set design. In the 1950s he travelled to London and Sweden where he began writing. He spent several years in Australia after that, returning to his native city in 1972. His plays include *Countrywoman*, *The Stubborn Season* and *Stravanga*. He was awarded the American Irish Foundation Literary Award in 1978, and was a member of Aosdána. He is buried in Mount Jerome and there's a stone memorial to him near the Grand Canal, close to Charlemont Street, where he grew up.

Annie M P Smithson
1873-1948

Born in Claremont Road, Sandymount, Annie Mary Patricia Smithson lived in numerous locations around the city, from Harcourt Street and Rathmines to Nassau Street, Harold's Cross and Pembroke Street, before ending her days back in Rathmines. A midwife and district nurse, she trained at St Patrick's Nursing Home at 10 St Stephen's Green, (no longer there), and then worked tirelessly among the poor families of Dublin, many of whom lived around the now demolished tenements of York and Mercer Street. Although she didn't start writing seriously until she was in her forties she left behind a considerable portfolio of over twenty published novels, many involving doctor/nurse relationships, inspired perhaps by her own heartache when she fell in love with a married man, Dr James Manton. They corresponded for a long time and when she converted to Catholicism she burnt his letters. She became a fervent Republican and Nationalist and a member of Cumann na mBan. She never married and died in Richmond Hill, Dublin. She is buried in the grounds of Whitechurch Parish Church near Ballyboden. One of her best-known books is *The Marriage of Nurse Harding*, which is set during the Irish Civil War.

Gerry Smyth
1951-

Poet Gerard Smyth was born in the Liberties in Dublin's inner city, a childhood which greatly influenced his writings, which prompted poet Michael Hartnett to pronounce , 'Gerard Smyth is essentially a city-poet; lyrical, passionate ... he may do for Dublin in verse what Joyce did for it in prose.' He had his first poems published in the *Irish Press* by the literary editor David Marcus. He worked as a journalist with *The Irish Times*, where he was poetry critic at one stage. He is now responsible for the arts coverage as well as holding the role of managing editor. His works include such

Excerpt from AMELIA, Siobhan Parkinson
(The O'Brien Press, 1993)

'... Amelia and Mama were on the tram, swaying through Rathmines, over the canal at Portobello, down Camden Street and Dame Street, skirting the gates of Trinity College and on past the Houses of Parliament, over the Liffey to Sackville Place and the Pillar.

The air was fresh and sweet with spring as they left Kenilworth Square, and it gradually filled with the thronging sounds of the city as they approached the river. Sackville Street itself was alive with people scurrying about their business, but none of them, Amelia was sure, were on such happy business as she and her mama.

Inside Clery's it was warm and muffled, after the noisy street. The lady shop assistants wore black skirts with deep belts and trim white blouses, and they all wore their hair neatly pinned up. Some of the more dashing ones wore neckties, like men. A gentleman with an enormous moustache and an ebony cane paced up and down, keeping an eye out for shop-lifters, pick-pockets and trouble-makers.

In the fabric department, they were served by an assistant with a linen measuring tape around her neck. She rolled out bolts of material with a flick of her wrists. The silks and satins and lacy materials cascaded in glorious colours over the counters.'

collections as *World Without End*, *Loss and Gain*, *A New Tenancy* and *The Fullness of Time: New and Selected Poems* (Dedalus, 2010). He is a member of Aosdána.

James Stephens
1880-1950

Poet James Stephens was born in the Dublin Liberties. His family lived at 5 Thomas Court, before moving to 5 Artisan's Dwellings off Buckingham Street. His father died when he was just two and they moved again to 8 St Joseph's Road off Prussia Street. A hungry and ill-cared-for boy of just six, he was sentenced to the Meath Protestant Industrial School for Boys on Carysfort Avenue in Blackrock for begging. Here the children were not known by their names, but by a number, and

James was allocated 279. He was one of the lucky ones. He made friends with two brothers, Tom and Dick Collins, who had been placed in care not for any misdemeanours but because their father was ill. Their mother lived in Dun Laoghaire and she often invited James home with her boys. When his ten years at The Meath ended, James boarded with this family, who by then were living at 30 York Road. He taught himself shorthand and typing and began writing. He sent stories and poetry to several magazines and papers and his writing began to get noticed. AE published his poetry and he made his mark with *The Charwoman's Daughter*, first published serially in the *Irish Review*. This is a harrowing account of tenement life in Dublin and of how the only survival route lies in dreams. He also wrote *Etched in Moonlight*, *Here are the Ladies* and *The Crock of Gold* and an eyewitness account of the events of the Easter Rising entitled *The Insurrection* in Dublin. Stephens spent nine years as Registrar of the National Gallery in Merrion Square, but resigned in 1924, went to the States to lecture and moved to England, where he remained until his death. He is buried in St Andrew's, in Kingsbury, London.

Bram Stoker
1847-1912

Bram Stoker (left) was born in 15 Marino Crescent. It is said that his fertile imagination was nourished by tales of horror, told to him by his mother, when he was a sickly child. In 1878 he married Florence Balcombe in St Anne's Church, Dawson Street. Florence had previously been courted by his friend Oscar Wilde. This caused a bit of a rift when Oscar heard about it, but later Bram was one of the few of Wilde's friends who stood by him and visited him in exile after his prison sentence.

Although Bram Stoker wrote of other things in other books, it is because of his blood-curdling creation about an aristocratic vampire, *Count Dracula of Transylvania*, that most people remember his name. The sequel, *Dracula's Guest*, didn't appear for another seventeen years, two years after the author had died.

The book inspired countless films; the first was released in Germany in 1922 without permission, under the title *Nosferatu*, and its characters had all been given different names. As executor of her husband's estate,

Florence entered into a legal battle that saw a protracted law case ensue. The outcome was that she was to be given every copy that had been made of the film. She had these destroyed, but it is believed a few survived. The *Dracula* stories are said to have inspired over 1,000 films worldwide.

Stoker's ashes lie along with those of his son, Noel Thornley Stoker in the Columbarium at Golder's Green, London.

Eithne Strong
1923-99

Like so many of her contemporaries Eithne (O'Connell) Strong moved to Dublin to join the civil service and it was there she wrote *An Glor*, her first poems. While courting her more senior, Protestant, husband-to-be, her very Catholic parents came from Limerick and 'kidnapped' her taking her back home with them. She later 'escaped' and came back to Dublin to marry Rupert Strong, (cousin of L A G Strong). Together they founded Runa Press, which published poetry in both Irish and English. Her works include *Flesh – the Greatest Sin*, *An Sagart Pinc* and *My Daring Neighbour*. She also wrote several novels and based *The Love Riddle* on her forty-one-year marriage.

She is commemorated, with her husband, the psychoanalyst and poet Rupert Strong, by the Eithne and Rupert Strong Award for Best First Collection at the Poetry Now Festival in Dun Laoghaire, Co Dublin.

Francis Stuart
1902-2000

Francis Henry Montgomery Stuart was born in Queensland, Australia, but after his father's suicide when he was only an infant, his mother returned to Ireland, sending her son to boarding school at Rugby in England. In 1920 he became a Catholic and married Iseult Gonne, Maud Gonne's daughter. This didn't please Yeats, who had proposed to Iseult in 1917.

Both politically minded, Stuart and Gonne found themselves on the anti-Treaty side of the Civil War and he became involved in a gunrunning episode that went wrong, resulting in his internment. He began writing seriously after Independence, producing novels and poetry. However he conflicted with authority and public opinion again for his involvement and sympathies with the Nazis during WWII, when, estranged from his wife, he spent some years as a lecturer in Berlin University, helping to have German propaganda broadcast in Ireland. In 1945 Stuart decided to return to Ireland with a former student, Gertrude Meissner; they were unable to do so and were arrested and detained by Allied troops. After they were released, Stuart and Meissner lived in Germany and then France and England. They married after Iseult's death and returned to live in Dublin in 1958, where Stuart continued to write until his death at 97 years of age.

He produced over thirty books. *Black List Section H* is perhaps his best know work and is said to be autobiographical in parts. His last novel, *King David Dances*, appeared in 1996.

When Stuart was awarded the title Saoi by Aosdána it caused much controversy because of Stuart's past Nazi affiliations. Poet Máire Mhac An tSaoi tried to have him expelled from the organisation. He staunchly defended his standpoint and Máire Mhac an tSaoi subsequently resigned over the incident.

Jonathan Swift
1667-1745

Swift was born in the city centre at 7 Hoey's Court, where Little Ship Street stands today. His father had died several months before his birth and when Jonathan was only six he was sent off to Kilkenny College. He wasn't very happy there, no more than he was at Trinity College Dublin, and biographies often speculate that it was these formative years that led to the bouts of depression that plagued him all his life. On completion of his studies, which saw him leave with no great distinction but rather a 'special grace' degree, he went to England and took a post as secretary to Sir William Temple in Surrey while he prepared for ordination. Here he met Esther Johnson, 'Stella', before he was sent to minister in Carrickfergus. She followed him when her father died, with her chaperone cousin Ms Rebecca Dingley. Swift spent ten years in Trim, County Meath, before returning to London in a bid to advance his career. It was then he wrote *Journal to Stella* and started issuing anonymous pamphlets, quickly becoming the menace of the Establishment.

He spent much of his energies railing against injustice, corruption and hypocrisy in religion. He attacked England's policies for Ireland and berated the Irish for how they handled themselves. When he was returned to Ireland in 1713, he accepted the Deanery of St Patrick's Cathedral and remained there until his death. He also upped his pamphleteering activities, writing as

MB Drapier, in the persona of a Dublin shopkeeper. He opposed and succeeded in having copper coins minted by William Wood in England withdrawn from circulation in Ireland. The blind harpist Turlough O'Carolan, (1670-1738), wrote a satirical ballad in celebration of the failure of these coins. It's called *Squire Wood's Lamentation on the Refusal of his Halfpence.*

As Drapier, Swift also suggested, in *a Modest Proposal*, the eating of every fourth child of the poor to prevent them being a burden on the state! Some actually believed this was genuine. He managed to keep two women happy with *billets doux* and tender love poems. The second was another Esther, Esther von Homrigh, whom he called Vanessa. She was only thirty-six when she died and is buried at St Andrew's Church in Suffolk Street, now the home of Dublin Tourism. Stella died in her 46th year and is buried in St Patrick's Cathedral.

Swift was an avid gardener. He leased some grounds from the dioceses in which he grew such exotic produce as nectarines and peaches. The patch, called Naboth's Vineyard, was located on the grounds of the former Meath Hospital, Heytesbury Street.

He began to believe he was going insane, a sentiment shared by some of his friends. It is now widely believed that he suffered from the then unknown Meniere's disease. His last gesture was to leave his money for the foundation of St Patrick's Mental Institution, which was subsequently built at James's Street.

Swift was buried in St Patrick's Cathedral, according to his wishes – 'in the great aisle on the south side under the pillar next to the monument of Primate Narcissus Marsh, three days after my decease, as privately as possible, and at twelve o'clock at midnight.' He had also written his own epitaph – 'He has gone where savage indignation can lacerate his heart no more.' His grave is beside Stella's.

Swift is probably most famous

Above: Swift's death mask
Below: The title page from *The Works of Dr Jonathan Swift*

today as the author of *Gulliver's Travels*, originally known as *Travels into Several Remote Nations of the World by Lemuel Gulliver*. Although composed as a cutting attack on society, the book has worked its way into children's literature and continues in print in many illustrated editions. Scenes from the book of Gulliver with Lilliputians were commissioned to adorn some buildings in Bride Street, close to where Swift was born, worked, lived and died.

ST PATRICK'S HOSPITAL 1794

St Patrick's University Hospital was founded in 1 Bow Lane West, Dublin 8 as a home for the mentally ill by the bequest of Jonathan Swift. He drew up detailed plans and furnished his architect, George Semple, with painstaking instructions. He saw, more than 250 years ago, the need to establish proper care, treatment and protection for sufferers of mental illness. Swift knew what he was talking about – he had been found of unsound mind by a Commission of Lunacy in 1742. King George II granted a Royal Charter to the hospital in 1746. The hospital is still there and fully functioning, making it one of the oldest in the world.

He gave the little wealth he had,
To build a house for fools and mad,
And showed by one satiric touch,
No nation needed it so much.(Swift, *On the Death of Dr. Swift)*

SWIFT'S CONTEMPORARIES

Several contemporaries of Swift made names for themselves in the world of books and drama. Among these is **William Congreve** (1670-1729) who, although from England, moved to Ireland when his father was posted here. He was sent to Kilkenny College, where Jonathan Swift was already a pupil. It wasn't until they both found themselves at Trinity College that they became firm friends. He decided to study law but soon forsook this for his writings. An illness gave him time to start and he quickly produced several plays, including *Incognito*, *The Old Bachelor* and *The Double Dealer*.

Congreve also gave us two well know phrases:'*Music has charms to sooth a savage breast*' from *The Mourning Bride* (1697), and, also from the same play, '*Heaven has no rage like love to hatred turned, Nor hell a fury like a woman scorned.*' This is frequently paraphrased as 'Hell hath no fury like a woman scorned.'

Thomas Southerne

1659-1746 started life at Oxmantown Road before heading to London to continue his studies at the Middle Bar. He wrote several comedies for Drury Lane: *The Wive's Excuse* and *The Maid's Last Prayer*, which dealt with the social issues of women trapped in marriages to ineffective and unsuitable men. However, his tragedies, like *Oroonoko*, or *the Royal Slave* and *The Fatal Marriage* proved more enduring.

Richard Steele

1671-1729 was born close to St Patrick's Cathedral in Bull Alley Lane, of which there is no trace any more. Orphaned at an early age, an influential and benevolent uncle took care of his education, sending him to Charterhouse. He remained in England where he was involved with three periodicals of the time: *The Tatler*, *The Guardian* and *The Spectator*, which he co-founded with Joseph Addison. He was also a member of the famous Kit-Kat Club along with William Congreve. Steele wrote numerous plays – *The Lying Lover*, *The Christian Hero*, *The Conscious Lovers*, *The Tender Husband*. He also wrote comedies, even one with the unlikely title of *The Funeral*.

Another friend of Swift's was

Thomas Tickell

1686-1749 poet and man of letters, who was also a contributor to *The Guardian* and *Spectator*. He came to Dublin after graduating from Oxford. As Secretary to the Lords Justice he had his own apartment in Dublin Castle. In 1726 he married in nearby St James's Street Church and moved to the country for a while. On the family's return to Dublin they settled in a beautiful sylvan setting in Glasnevin where their next door neighbour at Delville was Dr Patrick Delany (see *Mary Pendarves Delany*). Unfortunately he didn't get to enjoy this beautiful setting for long. He died in England but was taken back to be buried at St Mobhi's Church, Glasnevin, where a plaque commemorates him. The Tickells' residence and the grounds now form part of the National Botanic Gardens, Glasnevin. His works include *On the Prospect of Peace*, *On the Death of Mr Addison*.

Mary (Pendarves) Delany

1700-88 was a social diarist and a socialite too. She visited Dublin for the first time in 1731, where she was a guest of the Claytons. He was Bishop of Killala and his townhouse at 80 St Stephen's Green was part of Iveagh House and now the Department of Foreign Affairs. Apart from extolling the charms of the magnificent house and its sumptuously appointed and decorative apartments in her missives and correspondences, she also wrote home about how her hosts '*kept a very handsome table,*

six dishes of meat are constantly at dinner, and six plates at supper.' She was accepted into Dublin's literary circle and met a Dr Delany, Dean of Down, who lived in Delville House, Glasnevin, now the site of the Bon Secours Hospital. His salons often included names like Dean Swift and Stella and when he was widowed he proposed to Mary. They lived in Glasnevin until he died; then she returned to London. Her biography and letters were published a few years after her death. She is buried in St James's Piccadilly, London.

Joseph Addison

1672-1719 Addison came to Ireland to take up lodgings at Dublin Castle, where he had been appointed Chief Secretary to the Lord Lieutenant in1708. While here he continued to write essays for *The Tatler*, which had been started by his aforementioned school friend Richard Steele. His literary interests soon put him in touch with Thomas Sheridan, grandfather of Richard Brinsley Sheridan, and he became Swift's confidant in the business of the Drapier's Letters. His other close friends were Dr Patrick Delany and Thomas Tickell. A commemorative plaque to Tickell in St Mobhi's Church, Glasnevin may seem an unlikely place to find a tribute to Addison, but it's there. It reads

'*Sacred to the memory of Thomas Tickell Esq. He was sometime under Secretary in England and afterwards for many years Secretary to the Lords Justices of Ireland: but his highest honour was that of having been the friend of Addison.*'

J M Synge
1871-1909

John Millington Synge was born in Newton Villas in Rathfarnham, but when his father died his mother moved to Orwell Park, Rathgar. He spent some time at Mr Harrick's Classical and English School at 4 Upper Leeson Street but was taken out of school at fourteen because of his delicate constitution. He was tutored privately to prepare him for matriculation to Trinity College. In the meantime he attended music lessons at the Royal Academy of Music at 36 Westland Row and achieved a scholarship in counterpoint. He played with their orchestra on occasions at the Antient Concert Rooms on Brunswick Street (later Pearse Street). The Synges moved

again, to 29 Croswaithe Park West, Dun Laoghaire, to be beside the eldest daughter who had now married.

When Synge graduated he went abroad for further musical studies but instead decided to focus on literature. Following surgery for the removal of a cancerous gland in his neck, he spent the next six winters in Paris and the summers in the Aran Islands, where there is now a Synge Museum in the cottage where he used to stay. Lady Gregory rejected his first play for the Irish Literary Theatre. But once he was accepted he wrote six memorable plays in the space of six years.

His first theatrical achievement came with *In the Shadow of the Glen* in 1903, the year before the Abbey Theatre opened. The next year he wrote *Riders to the Sea* and followed that with *The Well of Saints*. Synge moved from Dun Laoghaire to a flat at 15 Maxwell Road in Rathmines and from there to 57 Rathgar Road.

His next offering saw all hell break loose

during the performance of *The Playboy of the Western World*. The audience was scandalised by lines such as '*a drift of chosen females standing in their shifts*'. Despite this, the crowds kept turning up, some to catcall and heckle, and others to see the play for themselves. They were joined nightly by members of the local constabulary whom the theatre had called to keep the peace.

A young actress, Máire O'Neill, who used the stage name of Molly Allgood, had caught Synge's eye and they got engaged in 1907, but didn't make that news generally known. There was a fifteen-year age difference. They had planned to marry and had found a home at 47 York Road, but Synge's cancer returned and they never did. He was suffering from the then incurable Hodgkin's Disease and had to have more surgery. He went abroad against medical advice and while in Germany learned of his mother's death. When he had recovered sufficiently he returned to Ireland, but died four months later at the age of only 38. Synge had been working on *Deirdre of the Sorrows*

when he died and it was produced after his death.

He is buried in Mount Jerome Cemetery, with his parents. Molly Allgood didn't attend the funeral. Synge had known she wouldn't. While contemplating his pending demise he had obviously had such a discussion with her and then written this poem.

I asked if I got sick and died would you
With my black funeral go walking too
If you'd stand close to hear them talk and pray
While I'm let down in the steep bank of clay
And No, you said, for if you saw a crew
Of living idiots pressing round that new
Oak coffin – they alive, I dead beneath
That board – you'd rave and rend them with your teeth.

Below: A newspaper advertisement for Synge's *The Playboy of the Western World*

ABBEY THEATRE.

TO-NIGHT .. .. At 8.15.
First Production of
THE PLAYBOY OF THE WESTERN WORLD,
A Comedy in Three Acts, by J. M. Synge.
Preceded by
RIDERS TO THE SEA,
A Play in One Act, by J. M. Synge.
Stalls, 3s ; Balcony, 2s ; Pit, 1s and 6d. Booking at Cramer's.
20069

Molly Allgood's sister, a Mrs Callender, disapproved of the play, and presumably of her sister's role in it. Proving that he had a sense of humour, Synge responded in verse:

The Curse
To a sister of an enemy of the author's who disapproved of 'The Playboy'

Lord, confound this surly sister,
Blight her brow with blotch and blister,
Cramp her larynx, lung, and liver,
In her guts a galling give her.
Let her live to earn her dinners
In Mountjoy with seedy sinners:
Lord, this judgement quickly bring,
And I'm your servant, J.M.Synge.

Katharine Tynan
1861 -1931

Principally known for her poetry, Tynan was also a novelist. She was born in Dublin and lived by the Grand Canal at 25 South Richmond Street. When she was seven the family moved to Clondalkin, County Dublin, then in the heart of the countryside. Her new home was a house called White Hall where her parents entertained liberally and where Katharine came into contact with many literary personages of the day.

Despite poor sight she wrote copiously and had her first collection of poetry published when she was just seventeen. Over the years she became integrated into various literary circles and numbered W B Yeats, George Sigerson, John O'Leary, Douglas Hyde and Maud Gonne among her friends. She married a magistrate and moved to London where she continued to write, often as Katharine Tynan Hinkson. On returning to Ireland the family lived in Sorrento Terrace in Dalkey and in Corbawn Lane in Shanganagh Vale in Shankill, before following her husband to a new posting to Claremorris in Mayo. After his death she divided her time between Dublin and London, keeping homes at Killiney and in Shankill. She died in London and is buried in St Mary's Kensal Green Cemetery.

Her work includes over 100 novels, short story and poetry collections, plays and several volumes of memoirs and autobiography. Her novels include *A Mad Marriage*, *The Respectable Lady*, *Denise the Daughter* and *The Forbidden Way*.

There's a commemorative plaque in her honour at the

Dominican Priory in Tallaght, quite close to where she grew up in Clondalkin. This was unveiled by President Mary Robinson in 1993 and is inscribed with a stanza from Katharine Tynan's prayer and well known poem *Sheep and Lambs*.

Anthony Trollope
1815-82

Writer Anthony Trollope is regarded as one of the greatest Victorian novelists. The creator of the *Barsetshire Chronicles* and of *The Pallisers*, he had never written anything before he found himself being dispatched to Ireland after joining the Postal Service. He moved about quite a bit before spending five years in Dublin, living in Donnybrook at 6 Seaview Terrace. During his various sojourns he left many references to how much he enjoyed being in the country, where he found our 'working classes to be much more intelligent than those in England.' He produced a vast volume of work, from travel books and biographies to short stories and almost fifty novels, four of them set in Ireland. These were *The Macdermots of Ballycloran*, *The Landleaguers*, *Castle Richmond* and *The Kellys and the O'Kellys*.

He paid a manservant an extra £5 per annum to waken him up with a cup of coffee so that he could start working at 5am. He wrote for three hours every day and then went to work. When he died, rather than leaving his son money in his will, Trollope left him his autobiography and two novels ready for sale and publication!

'It is admitted that a novel can hardly be made interesting or successful without love ... it is necessary because the passion in it is one which interests or has interested all. Everyone feels it, has felt it, or expects to feel it.'
Trollope's autobiography

Enda Walsh
1967-

Dublin-born playwright Enda Walsh currently lives in London. He attended Greendale Community School, Kilbarrack, where Roddy Doyle and Paul Mercier both taught. He has written for stage screen and theatre, collecting quite a few trophies along the way. In 1997 he won the Stewart Parker and George Divine Awards and in 2006 he was given the Abbey Theatre Writer in Residence Award. He wrote *Sucking Dublin* for the Abbey Theatre Company and this was produced at the Samuel Beckett Theatre in Trinity College. His films include *Hunger*, *Chatrooms* and *Island of Aunts*.

LITERARY FIGURES ON IRISH STAMPS AND CURRENCY

Several of our writers have been commemorated over the years on Irish banknotes and postage stamps

Currency: The £10 note in use from 1982 to 1993 celebrated Dean Swift. The background showed a reproduction of the coat of arms of the city of Dublin taken from a city council resolution against a letter by Swift, dating from April 1735. The reverse reproduced a section from a map of the city published in 1756, detailing an area along the River Liffey from Great Abbey Street to Aston's Quay (now Middle Abbey Street and Aston Quay)

William Butler Yeats was the subject of a £20 note in the same series. It displayed the poet and dramatist alongside a representation of the mythological Queen Maebh, based on the motif used by the Abbey Theatre. The background featured some lines from a Yeats manuscript, entitled *Deirdre*.

The £10 in the series that was issued from September 1993 until 2000 honours James Joyce; the background features Dublin and Wicklow, particularly Dublin Bay.

The back of the note features one of the heads on The Custom House, Dublin by Edward Smyth. The head is one of fourteen and believed to represent the River Liffey. A nineteenth century map and part of *Finnegan's Wake* also feature.

Douglas Hyde's portrait graced the face of the £50 note from 1995 until the end of 2001. As first President of Ireland and founder of the Gaelic League his figure was set against the official presidential residence in the Phoenix Park, *Áras an Uachtaráin*. The reverse side of the note featured a seal of *Conradh na Gaeilge* (a body which fosters the Irish language) and an excerpt from a sixteenth century manuscript which is in the custody of the Royal Academy of Arts.

Stamps: In 1967 An Post issued a 300-year commemorative set of stamps to mark the anniversary of Dean Swift's birth in 1667. These depicted scenes from *Gulliver's Travels*.

In 2004 Sweden and Ireland issued postage stamps designed to honour the four Irish Nobel literature laureates: William Butler Yeats, George Bernard Shaw, Samuel Beckett and Seamus Heaney. Each had a separate stamp with his portrait. Shaw, Beckett and Yeats also appeared on a similar collection on Irish playwrights in 1994 and in 1980 and 2000.

In 1980 Wilde and Shaw featured in the Europa series of stamps, and in 2000, on the anniversary of Wilde's death, Oscar was given an elaborate set of four all to himself.

1999 saw a stamp for the centenary of Micheál MacLiammóir's birth, while Bram Stoker's centenary was marked with Dracula's image.

In May 2010, An Post issued a single stamp to commemorate the birth centenary of Máirtín Ó Direáin, who was born in Sruthán, Inis Mór, Aran Islands in 1910. He was the son of a small farmer and spoke only Irish until his mid-teens. He came to Dublin to work in the Civil Service and spent the rest of his life here. His autobiographical essays are collected as *Feamainn Bhealtine*. He was a member of Aosdána.

Isaac Weld
1774-1856

Isaac Weld was born on Fleet Street and educated at Samuel Whyte's Academy on Grafton Street. It's now the site of Bewley's café (*photo opposite*) and was also the alma mater of Richard Brinsley Sheridan, Arthur Wellesley, Duke of Wellington, artist George Petrie and Robert Emmet. Weld was one of Ireland's early travel writers, with a curiosity about other places and a need to know if the lore about them was true. He journeyed to America and Canada, partly as an adventure and partly to discover if such faraway places would be suitable for

the Irish to emigrate to. His verdict: '*Any part of those territories might be looked forward to as an eligible and agreeable place of abode*'. Despite this proclamation, when he returned in 1797 he said he was '*...without entertaining the slightest wish to revisit it.*' His travel writings were translated and published in Italian, Dutch, German and French. He is buried in Mount Jerome Cemetery.

Lady Jane Wilde
1821-96

Jane Francesca Agnes, Lady Wilde (born Jane Francesca Elgee) was a poet and translator, better known under her pen name of Speranza, as well as for being Oscar Wilde's mother. She was the niece of Rev. Charles Robert Maturin. Much of her early work appeared in *The Nation* and was of a nationalist nature. She married William Wilde, an extremely successful eye specialist, who was later knighted, adding even more spice and flamboyance to her legendary literary salons at Number 1, Merrion Square – now the American College. It took six servants, a French maid and a German governess to run the household and the children were home schooled until they were old enough to go to boarding school. However, a scandal involving one of her husband's female patients led to a much publicised court case and to the Wildes having to pay considerable damages. When Francesca's husband died there was little money left and the house was repossessed. She moved to England to live with her other son, Willie, and continued to write poetry and prose.

It wasn't long before scandal rocked their worlds again – this time Oscar was in the spotlight and subsequently imprisoned. Lady Wilde's wish was to be allowed to see her son once more before she died, but this was refused.

There's a memorial to Sir William Wilde and Lady Wilde and their offspring in Mount Jerome Cemetery, although she is buried in Kensall Green Cemetery in London and her children are elsewhere.

SIR WILLIAM ROBERT WILLS WILDE, 1815-1876, aural and ophthalmic surgeon, archaeologist, ethnologist, antiquarian, biographer, statistician, naturalist, topographer, historian, folklorist, lived in this house from 1855 to 1876.

Oscar Wilde
1854 -1900

One of the best-known Irish

Danny Osborne's flamboyant statue of Oscar
Wilde in Merrion Square, erected in 1977

OSCAR WILDE

writers, Oscar Wilde's quotations litter collections and websites, his plays are still performed, and his only novel, *The Picture of Dorian Gray* has been filmed on a number of occasions. He wrote nine plays, including *A Woman of No Importance*, *An Ideal Husband*, *Lady Windemere's Fan*, *The Importance of Being Earnest*. He was born at 21 Westland Row, now the Oscar Wilde Centre for Irish Writing at Trinity College, and christened Oscar Fingal O'Flahertie Wills Wilde. When he was just a year old the family moved to the much more fashionable and larger residence on the corner of Merrion Square, now the American College.

Oscar followed his older brother to the Portora Royal School in Enniskillen. He went on to win a scholarship to Trinity College where he shared rooms with his brother Willie, who had published several of his own poems in the College magazine *Kottabos*, which he also edited.

Oscar read the classics and won the highest award for Greek, the Berkeley Gold Medal. His tutor, John Pentland Mahaffy, and Robert Tyrrell, his Professor of Greek, influenced him greatly. Mahaffy and he became good friends, and together they explored the Greek Islands and parts of Italy. Wilde credited him with teaching him the art of conversation, a sentiment with which Mahaffy was happy to concur until after the scandals surrounding Wilde's personal life. Then Mahaffy declared that Wilde was 'the only blot on my tutorship'.

Wilde took up a scholarship to Magdalen College Oxford, where he read Greats from 1874-1978 and began his career as a writer. His poem *Ravenna* won the Sir Roger Newdigate Prize. However he had to cut short his studies at Oxford when his father died, leaving substantial debts and mortgages on a number of properties.

His brother was left 1 Merrion Square, but his mother left Ireland and moved into lodgings in London.

Oscar had been going out with Florence Balcombe but she turned down his advances to marry Bram Stoker, whom he had known at Trinity. Although upset, Oscar wrote, '... sending you my wishes that you may be happy; whatever happens I at least cannot be indifferent to your welfare; the currents of our lives flowed too long beside one another for that.'

He spent a year in the US in

1882 lecturing about the decorative arts. He wrote copiously, editing *Woman's World* magazine between 1887 and 1889. He married Constance Lloyd in 1884, whom he proposed to in Ely Place, Dublin, where her grandmother lived. Constance came from money and after their marriage and their Parisian honeymoon they lived in Tite Street, Chelsea, where their sons, Cyril and Vyvyan were born.

In 1888 he published *The Happy Prince and Other Tales*, fairy-stories for his boys. His novel, *The Picture of Dorian Gray*, followed in 1890.

Oscar was by then the darling of the salons – for his wit, humour, his eccentric dress and his penchant for wearing a green carnation in his lapel. Wilde's first stage success was *Lady Windemere's Fan* (1892) and he followed that up with *A Woman of No Importance* the following year. In 1895 *An Ideal Husband* wowed the audiences and in the same year he gave them perhaps his most famous play of all, *The Importance of Being Earnest*. He was the subject of a portrait by Toulouse Lautrec that year too.

After Yeats met Wilde at a party in London, he remarked, 'My first meeting with Oscar Wilde was an astonishment. I never before heard a man talking with perfect sentences, as if he had written them all overnight with labour and yet all spontaneous.'

Wilde's personal life had become a matter of rumour and innuendo and at the height of his triumph he launched an action for criminal libel against the Marquess of Queensbury. This collapsed and Oscar was immediately arrested for his intimate association with the Marquess's son, Alfred Douglas, or Bosie, as he was known. He was charged with acts of homosexuality and given two years hard labour for the crime of sodomy. He was sent to Wandsworth prison and then to Reading Gaol, where he wrote *De Profundis* and *The Ballad of Reading Goal* for Bosie. Two months after his trial he was declared bankrupt. His wife changed her name to Holland and took their sons to live in Italy.

Upon his release, Wilde went to live in exile in France. He changed his name to Sebastian Melmoth, after a character created by Charles

Maturin in *Melmoth the Wanderer*. He died in Paris on 30 November 1900 and was buried in Bagneux Cemetery. His remains were moved in 1909 to a tomb at Père Lachaise Cemetery, Paris. His elaborate tombstone is inscribed with a verse from his *Ballad of Reading Gaol*:

> *And alien tears will fill for him*
> *Pity's long broken urn*
> *For his mourners will be outcast men*
> *And outcasts always mourn.*

William Butler Yeats
1865-1939

Yeats was born in Sandymount, Dublin 4 into an artistic family. His father, John Butler Yeats, was a painter and his brother Jack B. became one of Ireland's most respected painters. Their two sisters were very active in the Arts and Crafts movement.

WB was educated partly in England and in Erasmus Smith High School, then in Harcourt Street. It's better known now as The High School and is in Rathgar. The Yeats family had numerous addresses around Dublin, from Gardiner Street to Howth. His father took a studio at 7 St Stephen's Green, where, it seems, he held court to all sorts of people who dropped in as he worked. Failing finances occasioned a move to 10 Ashfield Terrace, later renamed 418 Harold's Cross Road. AE was a frequent visitor there. W B and he had been students together at the Metropolitan School of Art in Kildare Street. The family moved back to England again and it was there that he met Maud Gonne, to whom he later proposed, more than once. She turned him down.

Yeats's first published work was a fantasy poem, *The Isle of Statutes*, which appeared in the *Dublin University Review*. It was followed by a collection called *The Wanderings of Oisín and Other Poems*.

Through his expanding literary connections and his annual visits to Lady Gregory at Coole Park in Sligo, he became one of the founders of the Irish Literary Theatre in Dublin in 1898. Six years later, established and successful, it graduated to its own permanent address as the Abbey Theatre, later still to become Ireland's National Theatre Company. The first plays were performed at the Antient Concert Rooms in Brunswick Street (now the Academy building in Pearse Street). As its main playwright, many of Yeats's works featured in the early days. The first was *The*

Countess Cathleen. His *Cathleen Ní Houlihan* had Maud Gonne as the leading lady. These were followed by *The Land of Heart's Desire* and *The King's Threshold*. During this time Yeats was occupied, along with one of his sisters, Elizabeth, in starting Dun Emer Press, which later became the Cuala Press, which closed down in 1910.

He married when he was 52 and his bride, George Hyde-Lees, had just turned 25. They had two children, Anne and Michael. At this point he was still living between two countries and when his children arrived he decided to move back to Ireland and bought a summerhouse

in County Galway, an old Norman Castle. They moved back to England only to return again when Yeats was elected to the Senate of the Irish Free State in 1922. He bought a house at 82 Merrion Square, within walking distance of Leinster House.

The following year he received the Nobel Prize in Literature. In 1924 he chaired a committee to decide on the designs of the first Irish currency and banknotes and was later honoured on a £20 note that was in circulation from 1982 to1993. He was re-elected to the Senate in 1925.

WB continued to write and his works include *The Second Coming,*

The Green Helmet, The Tower, Responsibilities, The Winding Stairs and New Poems, which was published the year before he died. He also wrote a book called A Vision, inspired by his mystical inclinations and his theosophical beliefs.

There's a bust of Yeats in Sandymount Green, close to where he was born. His last Dublin address was Riversdale House, an impressive 18th century farmhouse on Ballyboden Road, Rathfarnham. This inspired two of his poems - What Then? and An Acre of Grass. When plans were proposed to demolish the house on which Yeats had taken a 13-year lease in 1932, it met with much local resistance and in June 1999 South Dublin County Council added the house, along with its original gates, piers and arched bridge to its list of protected structures. It was here that Yeats met Maud Gonne McBride for the last time when she visited him in 1938.

He died in Mouton, in the south of France and was buried in Roquebrune-Cap-Martin, but later, as he had wished, he was brought home and re-interred in his beloved West of Ireland at Drumcliffe Cemetery in the shadow of Ben Bulben Mountain, about which he had written. His epitaph reads:-

Cast a cold eye
on life, on death.
Horseman, pass by!

Zozimus
1794-1846

Blind balladeer Michael Moran was known to all and sundry as Zozimus, after a bishop in one of his recitations. He was born at Faddle Alley, off Black Pitts, in the heart of Dublin Liberties. He later lived at 14 ½ Patrick Street. He had quite a following and he and his dog used to hold court on the corner of Carlisle Bridge (now O'Connell Bridge). As he couldn't afford a decent burial he worried that his body might be used to teach the students at the Royal College of Surgeons when he died. That fear wasn't realised. Instead he was placed in a pauper's grave in Glasnevin Cemetery. However, Dubliners have long memories, and in 1988, when the city celebrated its millennium, the Smith brothers of the Submarine Bar in Crumlin and the Dublin City Ramblers erected a handsome memorial on his grave. Its inscription reads:

Sing a song for aul Zozimus
As always from the heart
Your name will forever live
As a Dubliner apart.

Edward Delaney's 1966 Thomas Davis
memorial in College Green

The James Joyce Centre
35 North Great George's Street,
Dublin 1
www.jamesjoyce.ie
The Centre is located in a house that was built in 1784 and which has a link to Joyce through Professor Denis J Maginni who ran a Dance Academy there. Maginni was a well-known and colourful character in Dublin and he appears several times in *Ulysses.*

The building was saved from demolition by one of Dublin's foremost Joycean scholars, Senator David Norris (who has written the foreword for this book) and is a resident of the street. With the support of a resolute band of followers the building was spared and opened in 1996. The Centre organises lectures, exhibitions and a variety of events designed to promote a better understanding of the writer and his works. Ken Monaghan, a son of Joyce's sister, May, was involved in drawing up the Joyce Walking Tour route, which may be booked from the Centre along with other Joyce-related walks.

The Centre is a mecca for Joycean scholars and those with more than a passing interest in this quintessential Dubliner.

The James Joyce Museum
Joyce Tower, Sandycove,
County Dublin
Tel: (+353 1) 2809265
www.visitdublin.com
One of a series of Martello towers built to withstand an invasion by Napoleon, this now houses a museum devoted to the life and works of James Joyce, who made the tower the setting for the first chapter of *Ulysses.*

The museum's collection includes letters, photographs, first and rare editions and personal possessions of Joyce, as well as items associated with the Dublin of *Ulysses.*

Located eight miles south of Dublin city on the coast road, the museum can be reached by DART or bus. It is open from April to August.

The Irish Writers' Centre
19 Parnell Square, Dublin 1
www.writerscentre.ie
The Irish Writers' Centre, beside the Dublin Writers' Museum, has long been a hub of literary activity in the city, supporting established and

aspiring writers throughout the country. It's a non-profit organisation, aimed at promoting literature and writers in Ireland.

Since it was founded in 1991, the Centre has welcomed many award-winning writers through its doors, including Nobel, Costa, Man Booker, IMPAC and Pulitzer Prize winners. It has also served as an important platform for breakthrough talent, with many young writers giving their first public readings here.

Through a diverse programme of creative writing workshops, seminars, lectures and readings, the centre nurtures emerging talent and fosters relationships between writers and their Irish audience. The creative writing students benefit from the guidance and insight of successful, published poets, novelists, and short story writers.

Many writing groups use the Centre to hold their meetings, to exchange ideas and develop their writing. The staff also run a monthly book club, where the public are invited to come and be part of their thriving literary community.

Dublin Writers' Museum
18 Parnell Square, Dublin 1
www.writersmuseum.com

Among the pens, typewriters and smoking pipes there are some interesting personal curiosities on view at the Dublin Writers' Museum. Swift and Wilde, Shaw and Yeats, Joyce and Beckett are among those presented through their books, letters, portraits and personal items. Among the treasures you'll find Oliver St. John Gogarty's laurels, Lady Gregory's lorgnette, Austin Clarke's desk, Samuel Beckett's telephone, Mary Lavin's teddy bear. Brendan Behan's union card is there too, complete with his fingerprints, which were well known to the British and Irish constabularies. He also sent a postcard from Los Angeles with the message: '*Great spot for a quiet piss-up*'. There's a note from Sheridan to a creditor, and a signed refusal from George Bernard Shaw – to provide an autograph! The first edition of Patrick Kavanagh's *The Great Hunger* includes a stanza in his own handwriting, which the prudish publisher refused to print at the time. There's a room devoted to children's literature – *Seomra na nÓg*; the Gallery of Writers has busts and portraits of many well known and loved names and you'll find some first editions and out of print manuscripts in the Library.

The National Print Museum
Old Garrison Chapel, Beggars Bush,
Haddington Road, Dublin 4
www.nationalprintmuseum.ie
With so much literary talent about it should be no surprise to learn that Dublin is also home to the National Print Museum. Printing in its day was as revolutionary as computers were in the last century.

Nowadays poets and writers can write, erase, change, edit, crop and recompose with the touch of a key, producing print-ready tomes and collections. But it wasn't always so. Formerly, every single individual letter had to be picked from printers' trays and each word spelt backwards so that, when dipped in ink and printed on the paper, it would read correctly. These skilled acts were executed by compositors who worked in 'hot metal'.

The National Print Museum began in 1985, when new technology and computers were fast making old skills and large printing obsolete. Work commenced on saving machinery from this fast disappearing era. A committee representing all sections of the printing industry, including commercial printers, suppliers, newspapers, trade unions and academia, combined their knowledge to preserve this vital part of our literary heritage. The Office of Public Works donated the former Garrison Chapel in Beggars Bush Barracks, Dublin 4 to become the National Print Museum in 1991. It opened in 1996 and contains over 10,000 objects covering the whole range of the craft, including machinery, printing blocks, metal and wooden moveable type, photographs, books, pamphlets, periodicals and much more. The associated skills of bookbinding and stitching are also represented, as is a unique pen-ruling machine, used to line thousands of children's copybooks in which they learned to do 'joined-up' writing in times past.

It is well worth a visit.

DUBLIN LIBRARIES OF NOTE

Trinity College Library
Trinity College Dublin, College Green,
Dublin 2 www.tcd.ie/Library/
This wonderful library is as old as the College itself and was

in the UK – some 100,000 every year. The latest addition to Trinity's book bank is the €27 million eight storey high James Ussher Library.

Marsh's Library, St Patrick's Close, Dublin 8
www.marshlibrary.ie

Untouched by modernity, Marsh's Library, beside St Patrick's Cathedral in St Patrick's Close is truly a time machine, dating back to 1702. The oldest public library in Ireland, it was the brainchild of Archbishop Narcissus Marsh, who was at that time Provost of Trinity College. Many of the collections in the Library are still kept on the shelves allocated to them by Marsh and by Elias Bouhéreau, the first librarian, when the Library was opened.

established in 1592. It's the largest repository in the land, with a catalogue of over 5 million printed volumes, as well as music, journals, newspapers and an additional storage unit in Santry. The library is one of Dublin's most visited tourist attractions principally because it is the keeper of the world renowned illuminated manuscript, the Book of Kells. It also houses the Book of Durrow, believed to date from the seventh century, the Book of Armagh and the twelfth century Book of Leinster. In 1801 the Library was endowed with a legal deposit privilege meaning that it continues to receive copies of newly published material in Ireland and

The Library was formally incorporated in 1707 by an Act of Parliament called *An Act for settling and preserving a public library for ever.* The Act vested the house and books in a number of religious and state dignitaries and

officials and their successors as Governors and Guardians of the Library.

The interior of the library, with its beautiful dark oak bookcases with carved and lettered gables, remains unchanged since it was built three hundred years ago. It still has its three wired 'cages' where the readers were locked in when perusing rare books (*see photo overleaf*). It was frequented by Swift, who often made notes or comments in the margins. Charles Maturin wrote several of his books here and Carleton was a frequent visitor. Maturin's son later became a librarian there.

Muriel McCarthy, Keeper of the Library since 1989, wrote its history in *Marsh's Library - All Graduates and Gentleman*.

Chester Beatty Library
Dublin Castle, Dublin 2
www.cbl.ie

The Chester Beatty Library was named Irish Museum of the Year in 2000, the year it moved from Ballsbridge to the historic Clock Tower Building of Dublin Castle, and in 2002 it was awarded the title of European Museum of the Year.

A New Yorker, Sir Alfred Chester Beatty was born in 1875, a mining mogul who made his millions in Cripple Creek, Colorado. He moved to Dublin in the 1950s and became an honorary citizen of Ireland in 1957. He was given a state funeral when he died in 1968 and bequeathed his fantastic treasure trove to the State. It lives in Dublin, contributing to our continuing literary heritage.

Chester Beatty began amassing this considerable collection of manuscripts, drawings, rare books, miniature paintings, prints and decorative arts from an early age. Some of them date back to 2,700 BC and they showcase the diversity of the rich artistic treasures of the great religions and cultures. These span the globe from North Africa and Asia, to the Middle East and Europe. In this treasury you can enjoy the richness of Egyptian papyrus texts, intricately illuminated copies of the Qur'an (Koran) and the Bible, Irish, European, medieval and renaissance manuscripts.

National Library of Ireland
2/3 Kildare Street, Dublin 2
www.nli.ie
The National Library is a valued source for researchers. It's not a lending library but is open, free of charge, to anyone wishing to consult the collections for material not otherwise available through the public library service or an academic library. It opened in 1877 and still occupies the same prime site at number 2/3 Kildare Street. It boasts a really magnificent reading room too.

OTHER LIBRARIES

Central Catholic Church Library
www.catholiclibrary.ie
Dublin City Libraries and Archive
www.dublincitypubliclibraries.ie
Benjamin Iveagh Library Farmleigh
www.farmleigh.ie
National Archives HYPERLINK
www.nationalarchives.ie
Royal Hibernian Academy
www.royalhibernianacademy.ie
Royal Irish Academy
www.ria.ie

DUBLIN THEATRES

The Abbey Theatre
26 Lower Abbey Street, Dublin 1
www.abbeytheatre.ie

The Abbey Theatre was founded by W B Yeats and Lady Gregory in 1903. Its precursors were the Irish Literary Theatre 1899, and Frank and Willie Fay's National Dramatic Society. However, with patronage from Miss Annie Horniman, the Mechanic's Institute was purchased on Old Abbey Street and on December 27th 1904 the Abbey Theatre opened its doors there. Its importance as part of the Celtic Revival was seminal and as it developed it fostered and produced a long list of playwrights, many illustrious. WB Yeats's *On Baile's Strand* and *Cathleen Ni Houlihan* and Lady Augusta Gregory's *Spreading the News* and John Millington Synge's *In the Shadow of the Glen*, were all presented by the Irish national Theatre Society, which had Maud Gonne, Douglas Hyde and George Russell (AE) on its board with Yeats as its president. Many plays which went on to have success elsewhere were rejected by the board over the years – the likes of Denis Johnston's *The Lady Says No*, O'Casey's *The Silver Tassie*, and Brendan Behan's *The Quare Fella*, among them.

The Abbey burned down in 1951 and relocated temporarily to the Queen's Theatre in Pearse Street (no longer there). This temporary sojourn lasted fifteen years! In 1966 the company moved back to Abbey Street, to a brand new theatre, with the smaller Peacock Theatre below, and with this move came a new wave of playwrights - Brian Friel, Tom Murphy, Thomas Kilroy, Hugh Leonard and Bernard Farrell among them.

Olympia Theatre
72 Dame Street, Dublin 2
www.olympiatheatre.ie

The Olympia Theatre, or The Star of Erin Music Hall, as it was originally known, was built in 1879. It continues to thrive with variety, drama and musical concerts.

Gaiety Theatre
53/54 South King Street, Dublin 2
www.gaietytheatre.ie

The grand opening of the Gaiety Theatre in Dublin on 27 November

1871 was a glittering affair, attended by the Lord Lieutenant and the cream of Dublin society of the day. Amid glittering chandeliers, the splendour of the Victorian theatre was unveiled. It has been revamped and renovated many times since then, but still retains its old world charm. Outside, beneath the distinctive canopy, performers and playwrights associated with theatre have been celebrated with handprints cast in bronze and set in the pavement. There you'll find those of playwrights John B Keane and Brian Friel, and actors Anna Manahan and Niall Toibin.

Smock Alley Theatre
8 Exchange Street Lower, Dublin 2
www.smockalley.com
The Gaiety School of Acting is currently managing a 110-seat black box space on the former site of the Theatre Royal. They are working alongside Temple Bar Cultural Trust and the Department of Arts, Sport and Tourism to reinstate Smock Alley Theatre to its former glory.

The New Theatre
43 East Essex Street, Dublin 2
www.thenewtheatre.com
The New Theatre opened in 1997. You need to know where it is to find it – tucked away at the back of the Connolly Bookshop in Essex Street, in Temple Bar. There they hold play readings once a month and produce new works, allowing new writers and directors a chance to get their work to the stage.
'The New Theatre continues to make a significant and important contribution to Dublin's theatre ecology' - The Arts Council

The Gate Theatre
1 Cavendish Row, Dublin 1
www.gate-theatre.ie
The Gate was founded by Hilton Edwards and Micheál MacLiammóir in 1928 and opened with a production of Peer Gynt. That set the tone for this venue, which specialises in producing a contemporary Irish and international bill of fare. It became the first theatre in the world to present a retrospective of Samuel Beckett's nineteen plays. The Gate has a long association with Brian Friel, premiering many of his plays, and in 2009 it celebrated the playwright's 80th birthday with a critically acclaimed season of his works. The theatre shared its facilities for many years with Lord Longford's company, who leased it annually while the Gate went on tour.

LITERARY AWARDS

Awards are a regular feature of Dublin's literary calendar. Foremost in an exhilarating round of events is the **International IMPAC Dublin Literary Award**, **www.impacdublinaward.ie** now in its fifteenth year. One of Dublin City Council's most prestigious and successful initiatives, the nomination process for the Award is unique as nominations are made by libraries in capital and major cities throughout the world. Participating libraries can nominate up to three novels each year for the Award. It plays a key role in encouraging reading and writing from all corners of the globe.

Other awards include:

American Ireland Fund Literary Award **www.irlfunds.org**

Bisto Book of the Year **www.childrensbooksireland.com**

Davy Byrnes Irish Writing Award **www.davybyrnesaward.org**

Francis MacManus Awards **www.rte/radio1/francismacmanus**

IMRAM **www.poetryireland.ie/whats-on/imram.html**

Irish Book Awards **www.irishbookawards.ie**

Irish PEN/A.T. Cross Achievement in Literature **www.irishpen.com/award.html**

The Irish Times Poetry Now Award **www.poetrynow.ie/times.html**

Oireachtas Literary Awards **www.antoireachtas.ie**

P.J. O'Connor Awards **www.rte.ie/radio1/pjoconnorawards**

Poetry Aloud Poetry Speaking Competition **www.nli.ie**

RAI Children's Book Award **www.reading.ie/bookAwards**

The Rooney Prize **www.tcd.ie/OWC writers/rooney-prize.php**

LITERARY FESTIVALS

Dublin Book Festival
www.dublinbookfestival.com
The Dublin Book Festival, established in 2008, has quickly become one of the most important literary happenings in Dublin. The Festival is intended to showcase, support and develop Irish publishing. Events are held throughout the city, at sites from City Hall to the National Library of Ireland.

In 2011, the Festival expanded from three to five days, including more than 40 events and more than 80 Irish authors. The festivities include book readings, discussions, and activities relating to children's books. This festival has been sponsored by various organizations, including the Arts Council and *The Irish Times.*

Dublin Writers Festival
www.dublinwritersfestival.com
The Dublin Writers Festival has been part of the city's cultural calendar over the past dozen years. It takes place at venues which include the National Concert Hall, Project Arts Centre and the Abbey Theatre. It's the capital's premier literary event celebrating the very best of Irish and international writers.

The six-day literary Festival features over 40 writers who read from their most recent works and take part in curated conversations about their writing. This festival is an initiative of Dublin City Council Arts Office and is supported by The Arts Council.

OTHER BOOK AND LITERARY FESTIVALS

Children's Book Festival
www.childrensbooksireland.com
Dublin: One City, One Book
www.dublinonecityonebook.ie
Bloomsday and Bloomsweek
www.jamesjoyce.ie
Poetry Now Festival
www.poetrynow.ie
Dun Laoghaire Rathdown – Mountains to Sea Book Festival
www.mountainstosea.ie
Dalkey Book Festival
www.dalkeybookfestival.org

LITERARY ORGANISATIONS

Children's Books Ireland (CBI)
www.childrensbooksireland.ie
iBbY (International Board on Books for
Young People) **www.ibbyireland.ie**
ILE (Ireland Literature Exchange)
www.irelandliterature.com
Publishing Ireland (The Irish Book
Publishers' Association)
www.publishingireland.com
The Arts Council **www.artscouncil.ie**

LITERARY WALKS

Dublin Tourism,
The Dublin Tourism Centre, Suffolk
Street, Dublin 2
(**www.visitdublin.com/seeanddo/tours/
guidedwalkingtours**) have suggestions for
a wide range of guided walking tours of
the city, including a Dublin Literary Pub
Crawl and an In the Steps of Ulysses
iWalk, one of a series of iWalks that are
free podcast audio guides to help you
discover Dublin at your own pace. The
Ulysses iWalk lets you explore the world
of James Joyce's masterpiece by visiting
the sights and scenes of the famous
novel. You can download the free iwalk
at **www.visitdublin.com/iwalks**.

James Joyce Walking Tours

The James Joyce Centre, 35 North Great
George's Street, Dublin 1, offers a variety
of Joyce-themed walking tours of Dublin
city. Visitors can follow in the footsteps
of Leopold Bloom by walking the route
he takes in the 'Lestrygonians' episode of
Ulysses, or take in some of the places
mentioned in the stories in *Dubliners*.
Whatever your interest in Joyce, there's a
tour that will suit you. Tours start from
the Joyce Centre and normally last about
90 minutes. Private and group tours can

also be organized. Check the Centre's
website at **www.jamesjoyce.ie** or email
your query to info@jamesjoyce.ie; Tel:
(+353 1) 8788547

Dalkey Castle & Heritage Centre, Castle
Street, Dalkey, Co Dublin Tel (+353 1)
2858366 offers guided literary walks to
settings in the work of James Joyce,
George Bernard Shaw, Flann O'Brien and
Hugh Leonard. Also covers Maeve Binchy
and Joseph O'Connor. (Must be pre-
booked, with a minimum number of six).
There is a Joycean Literary Walk in
Dalkey on Bloomsday, 16 June, annually.

BOOK FAIRS AND MARKETS

Antiques Fairs Ireland
www.antiquesfairsireland.com
Dublin City Book Fair
www.dublincitybookfair.com
Temple Bar Book Market
www.templebar.ie

Bibliography...

Alger, J and Smeaton, A, ed. *Dublin UNESCO City of Literature 2009, Dublin, 2009*, City of Dublin

Barrett, B, and Power, F, *The Golden Book of Dublin*, Dublin, 2003, The O'Brien Press

Bateson, R, *The End, Graves of Irish Writers*, County Meath, 2004. Irish Graves Publications

Bateson, R, *Dead and Buried in Dublin*, 2002, County Meath, Irish Graves Publications

Bolger, M, *Darting About*, Dublin, 2005, Ashfield Press

Bolger, M, *Dublin's Magical Museums*, Dublin 2008, Ashfield Press

Bolger, M, *Statues & Stories*, Dublin 2006, Ashfield Press

Bowen, E, *The Shelbourne*, Great Britain, 2001, Vintage Classics

Cowell, J, *Dublin's Famous People and where they lived*, Dublin, 1980, The O'Brien Press

Delaney, F, *Betjeman Country*, Great Britain, 1983, Hodder and Stoughton

Dictionary of Irish Biography, RIA, Dublin

Eyewitness Travel Dublin pocket map and guide, Great Britain, 2007, DK

Fennell, D, Bloomsway – *A day on the life of Dublin*, Dublin, 1990, Poolbeg Press Ltd

Frommer's Dublin Day by Day, Great Britain, 2008, Frommer's Travel Guides

Gonzalez , A, *Irish Women Writers – A- Z* . USA, 2006, Greenwood Press

Healy, E, *Elizabeth Healy's Literary Tour of Ireland*, Dublin, 1995, Wolfhound Press

Igoe, V, *A Literary Guide to Dublin*, London, 1994, Methuen

Igoe, V, *James Joyce's Dublin Houses*, Great Britain, 1990, Mandarin

Jeffares, A Norman, *Pocket History of Irish Writers*, Dublin, 1997, The O'Brien Press

Kostick, C, and Collins, L, *The Easter Rising – A Guide to Dublin in 1916*, Dublin, 2002, The O'Brien Press

Lalor, B, *Ultimate Dublin Guide*, Dublin, 1991, The O'Brien Press

Maine, G.F, ed. *The Works of Oscar Wilde*, Great Britain 1948, Collins

Malone, A, *Historic Pubs of Dublin*, Dublin, 2001, New Island Books

McCormack, J, *Story of Dublin*, Dublin, 2000, Mentor Books

O'Connor, U, *The Gresham Hotel* 1865-1965, Dublin

O'Neill, C, *Cathal O'Neill's Dublin*, Dublin 1998, Marino Books

Pearson, P, *Dun Laoghaire-Kingstown*, Dublin 1991, The O'Brien Press

Pearson, P, *The Heart of Dublin*, Dublin, 2000, The O'Brien Press

Roche, A, ed. *The UCD Aesthetic - celebrating 150 years of UCD Writers* , Dublin, 2005 New Island

Ryes, H, Ed. *Dublin, Perfect Gems of City Writing*, Great Britain, 2010, Oxygen Books

Tomedi, *J, Bloom's Literary Guide to Dublin*, New York, 2007, Checkmark Books

Quilligan, C, *Dublin Literary Pub Crawl*, Dublin, 2008, Writers' Island